Unfolding Daniel's Prophecies

Unfolding Daniel's Prophecies

Roy Allan Anderson

PACIFIC PRESS PUBLISHING ASSOCIATION

Mountain View, California
Omaha, Nebraska
Oshawa, Ontario

DEDICATION

To my son Allan whose scholarship and fellowship have oft inspired my pen.

INTRODUCTION

This book, *Unfolding Daniel's Prophecies*, has been long awaited by the readers of Dr. Anderson's excellent *Unfolding the Revelation*.

No book in the field of Biblical prophecy could be more timely than this work on Daniel's prophecies for two reasons: First, there is a strong feeling among students of Biblical prophecy that Daniel and the Revelation are understood best when studied together. Each needs the other. Second, the times in which we now live demand a restudy of the prophecies of Daniel.

The great prophetic cinema of the march of the ages moves with gathering speed before our eyes. We need a fresh approach, a re-study of the prophecies of Daniel which have been such a blessing to God's people since the days of the prophet himself. This is what this author has brought to us. Religious confusion reigns in our day; we need a clear understanding of the book of Daniel. One special strength of this book is the thorough research the author has made into the historical background of Daniel, the man and the book.

During his boyhood the prophet witnessed the collapse of the mighty Assyrian Empire which had dominated the Near East for centuries. He also saw the rise of the new Babylonian Empire under Nebuchadnezzar the Great. The invasions of the West, the capture of Jerusalem, and the forced transfer of the inhabitants to Babylon are graphically pictured. The prophet himself was one of these captives. Thus began the seventy-year captivity of God's people as predicted by Jeremiah. (See chapter 25:11, 12.)

Located at the very center and headquarters of the first prophetic world empire, Daniel wrote his great book on historic prophecy.

For several generations now Biblical scholars have disputed certain interpretations in the book of Daniel. Dr. Anderson's treatment of these issues is like a breath of fresh air on the subject. The historical credibility for the book of Daniel is especially emphasized in the chapter entitled, "Daniel in the Critics' Den." Here we see how modern archaeology has helped rescue the book of Daniel from its tormentors. A new understanding, a brilliant light, now penetrates many dark places of the past. Not only the existence but the identity of Belshazzar is clear. Important material on Darius and the friendship of Cyrus with Daniel will intrigue the reader.

Just before the first advent of Christ, the book of Daniel proved of great importance, identifying as it does the long expected Messiah. The prophecy of the seventy weeks found in Daniel, chapter 9, positively identifies Jesus of Nazareth as the true Messiah, the Christ of the Holy Scriptures. However, Daniel 9 is only a part of a larger prophecy which actually begins in chapter 8. Its complete fulfillment reaches down to the period just before the second coming of Christ, the period Daniel speaks of as "the time of the end." The author of this volume believes that we are now living in that time.

Again, the book of Daniel becomes important because, while the prophecies of that great book do not give a definite date for Christ's second coming, they do reach down with awe-inspiring accuracy to the very days in which we live. The eleventh chapter of Daniel, with its remarkable fulfillment in history, has always proved a problem to exegetes. This author makes a strong case for his enlarged view. That this prophecy of Daniel 11 has been fulfilled by the literal events of history has been generally accepted by Bible students at least down to verse 36. After presenting the conflict between the rulers of Alexander's broken empire and their followers, the author then shows how the Republic of Rome, with Julius Caesar and other great men from the West, played a prominent part in subsequent history. The words recorded in Daniel have been fulfilled with marvelous accuracy.

Finally, in Daniel 11:36 to 12:4, the author sees a greater fulfillment than have many writers in the past. He envisions a worldwide application of these verses. The Ottoman Empire passed away in 1922 after allied intervention in the Turkish war on Greece. But

Islam today is in the news. Mighty world changes are now taking place. New lineups and new divisions presage the time when demon spirits will take possession of human powers. These developments could lead to global government. Then the "dragon," "the beast," and the "false prophet" mentioned in the book of Revelation will have their day challenging the people of God.

Tensions in the East and Near East, with growing world confusion, seem destined to lead into world conflict until at last the voice of God in heaven declares, "It is done." Then His judgments will be poured out in seven-fold affliction which will surely bring the great confederacy of evil to collapse. As Daniel predicted, "He shall come to his end, and none shall help him."

The author wisely urges that we tread softly on unfulfilled prophecy. Remember the words of Jesus in John 13:19, "Now I tell you before it come, that, when it is come to pass, ye may believe that I am he." See also John 14:29.

From beginning to end, this book stresses the importance of the study of the prophecies of Daniel by everyone privileged to be living in these "latter days." Earnest study of God's Word will bring blessing and spiritual growth through the grace of our Lord Jesus Christ. Only the power of His divine Spirit can give us what is needful in our preparation to meet the King in His glory with peace and joy.

H. M. S. Richards, Sr.

PREFACE

Sir Isaac Newton, the great physicist, once said: "To reject Daniel is to reject the Christian religion."

A helpful study guide to the book of Daniel is Uriah Smith's work, *The Prophecies of Daniel and the Revelation*. It was written over a hundred years ago, and much more is known today. The discoveries of recent times give one a different outlook on the Babylon of Daniel's day. Much light has been shed on that ancient world. Events and geographical places, which earlier critics and liberal theologians declared must be fictitious, have today been proved accurate and true.

Knowledge concerning Babylon has increased, thus giving us an overview not available to people of previous generations. But Daniel wrote more than history; half of his book is prophecy. And next in importance to a saving knowledge of our Lord and Saviour is a knowledge of His prophetic program for our age and the coming age.

The world is being shaken to its foundations; civilization balances on the brink; "men's hearts [are] failing them for fear, and for looking after those things which are coming on the earth." For these times our Lord admonishes us to study "Daniel the prophet." He said, "Whoso readeth, let him understand." Matthew 24:15. Only those who understand the prophecies of Daniel and the Revelation can comprehend the issues we face in our generation. Daniel is the outstanding apocalypse of the Old Testament, as Revelation is of the New Testament.

Three times Daniel was called "greatly beloved" by Gabriel, the messenger of the God of heaven. One whose inspired counsel has meant much to us has well observed that "the book of Daniel is unsealed in the revelation to John, and carries us forward to the last scenes of this earth's history." "The light that Daniel received from God was given especially for these last days." "There is need of a much closer study of the word of God; especially should Daniel and the Revelation have attention as never before in the history of our work."—*Testimonies to Ministers,* pages 112, 113, 115.

"The Holy Spirit has so shaped matters, both in the giving of the prophecy and in events portrayed, as to teach that the human agent is to be kept out of sight, hid in Christ, and the Lord of heaven and His law are to be exalted. Read the book of Daniel. Call up, point by point, the history of the kingdoms there represented. Behold statesmen, councils, powerful armies, and see how God wrought to abase the pride of men, and lay human glory in the dust."—*Ibid.,* p. 112.

To deal with every facet in the book of Daniel and keep within the scope of these chapters is not possible. But I hope that those who read these pages will do so with hearts bowed in humility and prayer, asking that the Holy Spirit, whom the author believes has guided in the research, may lead the reader to a deeper knowledge of Daniel's God. Praise be to His name!

Roy Allan Anderson

TABLE OF CONTENTS

1. Who Was Daniel the Prophet?   13

2. Daniel at the Court of Babylon   22

3. Daniel in the Critics' Den   31

4. Prophetic Panorama of History to Be   41

5. The Mystic Stone Kingdom   54

6. Treason, Trial, and Triumph   62

7. Maniac King Regains His Kingdom   68

8. Belshazzar and Babylon's Fall   77

9. Cartoon Prophecies of World Empires   87

10. Antichrist and Heaven's Judgment   97

11. Daniel's Key Theme—The Sanctuary and Salvation   109

12. Messiah's Ministry and Predicted Day of His Death   118

13. Divine Intervention in International Politics   125

14. Political Intrigue Divides Greek Empire   130

15. Prophecy's Forecast of Rome's Rulership   137

16. Daniel Views Rise of Persecuting Powers   146

17. The Atheistic Revolution   152

18. Could Socialism Lead to World Government?   168

19. Righteous Shine as the Stars Forever   174

1
Who Was Daniel the Prophet?

Daniel holds a place of unusual honor in sacred history. Of all the ancient Hebrew writers this prophet-statesman stands out as unique. Not only did he profoundly influence his own generation, but his prophecies still have influence. His messages can mean even more to our own generation, living as we do just prior to our Lord's return.

Guided by the Holy Spirit, Daniel introduced a new type of revelation which we speak of as apocalyptic prophecy. Rather than giving glimpses of isolated events, this kind of prediction takes in the whole sweep of history from ancient times to the end of the age. The book of Daniel is up-to-date; certain parts read like the headlines in our morning papers. Truly Daniel is the prophet for our day.

Jesus referred to him as "Daniel the prophet" and added, "Whoso readeth, let him understand." As Fenton translates it, "Let the reader comprehend." Matthew 24:15.

To comprehend the messages of Daniel we need to know something of the international scene of his day. The opening words of his book are significant: "In the third year of the reign of Jehoiakim king of Judah came Nebuchadnezzar king of Babylon unto Jerusalem, and besieged it. And the Lord gave Jehoiakim king of Judah into his hand." Daniel 1:1, 2. Note that "the Lord *gave* Jehoiakim into his hand."

The year was 605 B.C., and this was the first of three invasions of Judah by the Chaldean conquerors. Daniel and his companions, the only exiles mentioned by name, were among those first taken to Babylon. The second invasion occurred in 598, when a much larger group was deported. Among them was a young priest, Ezekiel, who later wrote the book that bears his name. In the final invasion, in 586, the last large group of exiles, together with the remaining temple treasures, were taken to Babylon. Then the invading army destroyed Solomon's magnificent temple and the city of Jerusalem.

Tragedy in Jerusalem

Those were tragic days for the Jews. What would we have thought had we been there witnessing wave after wave of heathen armies carrying away the strongest of the people as slaves and leaving the city of Jerusalem a heap of ruins? Fear and grief filled the hearts of the Jewish people as they saw their lavish house of worship, probably one of the most ornate and beautiful buildings the world had ever known, leveled to the ground. Such a thing need never have happened had the nation heeded the messages of God through the prophets, especially Jeremiah. Daniel was not more than eighteen years of age—just a teen-ager—when he was snatched from his home and marched at least 800 miles to Babylon, the capital of idolatry. As far as we know, none of those first exiles ever saw his homeland again. The date of Daniel's birth could not have been later than 623 B.C. This coincided with the rise of the Neo-Babylonian kingdom, which, having conquered the warring empire of the Assyrians, quickly gained world renown.

Sunset of Assyrian Rule

The last strong king of Assyria was Ashurbanipal, who died in 626 or possibly as early as 631 B.C. The last remnants of Assyrian power collapsed during the reign of the weak king Ashur-uballit, when the Babylonians marched against Syria to quiet a revolt there. Later they attacked Egypt in order to overthrow all opposition to the establishment of Babylon's universal rule.

These campaigns against Syria and Egypt were entrusted to Nebuchadnezzar, the crown prince of the expanding Neo-Babylonian Empire. Right at the time he was ready to invade Egypt, word reached him that his father Nabopolassar had died. He therefore hurried home to Babylon by the shortest route in order to secure to himself the throne, leaving some of his generals to superintend the march of the captives, including Daniel, over the long, 800-mile journey to Babylon.

Three years earlier, in 608 B.C., King Josiah, one of Judah's greatest leaders, had been fatally wounded on the field of battle close to Megiddo. During his long reign this noble king had done much to lead the nation back to God. He sought diligently to undo the trend toward heathenism of the fifty-seven shameless years of the two kings before him—his grandfather Manasseh and his father Amon.

The Lost Book Sparks Great Revival

Josiah came to the throne when but a boy of eight years. At sixteen he was soundly converted, and two years later he led one of the most far-reaching revivals in the history of the nation. He then gave orders to repair the temple, which had then stood for four centuries. While the workmen performed their tasks, they found the "book of the law." It had evidently been placed in one of the pillars of the temple. They brought it to Shaphan, the scribe, who took it to the king. Hearing the reading of the word of the Lord, Josiah was alarmed. In humility he called a convocation of the leaders of the nation. As they came together and listened to the book of the covenant, they, too, were convicted; and, following the lead of the king, they laid plans which resulted in the greatest Passover service ever recorded. 2 Kings 23:21-23 and 2 Chronicles 35:1-9.

Daniel was but a child at the time of this national revival, the effect of which, under King Josiah's leadership, carried over for many years. When this leader fell on the field of battle in 608 B.C. and his body was brought home for burial, Daniel was a youth of fifteen years. It is not hard to imagine the impression this tragedy had on his adolescent mind. A short time later the whole nation entered into a memorial lament in Josiah's honor. Their sorrow was deep and lasting. But, sad to say, the effect of Josiah's devotion had little or no influence on his own sons.

A remnant of the nation's youth, however, remained true. Among these were young men of royal birth. Daniel and his companions were probably students in the Jerusalem school of the prophets, and may have studied the Hebrew Scriptures under the guidance of leaders like Habakkuk, Jeremiah, Zephaniah, and Nahum. At any rate, they were "skilful in all wisdom." Daniel 1:4.

The godly prophets and teachers bore witness for God and warned the people of coming national calamity. But apostate kings and false prophets opposed the messengers of the Lord and led the nation deeper into sin and idolatry until there was no remedy. See 2 Chronicles 36:14-16. Picture faithful Jeremiah going up and down the streets of Jerusalem wearing a yoke around his neck—a symbol of the tragedy that awaited the nation because of its defiant disobedience. He knew that the flower of its youth was destined to be captives and slaves in an alien land. But the leaders of the people gave little heed.

Daniel and friends probably knew of the experiences of Hezekiah as recorded in Isaiah 39. Because of that king's vanity in showing the ambassadors from Babylon the treasures of his kingdom, when he should have been giving glory to God and leading these visitors to a knowledge of Jehovah, Isaiah declared that his posterity would be "eunuchs in the palace of the king of Babylon." Isaiah 39:7. We can almost hear godly teachers like Habakkuk saying, "Young men, this could and may well happen to you. But if you determine to be true and faithful to God, no matter what happens, He will make you strong witnesses for truth and righteousness, even in wicked Babylon."

Separation From Families and Teachers

When at last the Chaldeans came, we can imagine these earnest teachers throwing an arm around these boys as they said farewell, wishing them God's blessing as they witnessed for Him in an alien land. Try to imagine these young men, under the cruel command of their captors, beginning their long trek to the great metropolis. That surely would have been a tragic sight. But for Daniel and his three dedicated friends the challenge became their opportunity.

Their parents and teachers had prepared them well for whatever awaited them. Josiah's godly influence was, unfortunately, lost on his own sons, Jehoahaz, Jehoiakim, and Zedekiah, and his grandson, Jehoiachin, each of whom became king for a short time and each of whom chose to follow his own wicked way. While the effects of

Josiah's revival were lost on his own sons, they were not lost on Daniel, Hananiah, Mishael, and Azariah, all of whom moved on to leadership even in the land of their servitude. The record of their fidelity to principle while facing sentences of death is recorded not only in the Old Testament; these men are mentioned by inference in Hebrews 11:33, 34 as men of faith.

Shortly after the death of Ashurbanipal, Nabopolassar, father of Nebuchadnezzar and commander-in-chief of the Chaldean armies in Babylonia, sensing the weak leadership of Ashurbanipal's sons, saw an opportunity to build up the ancient kingdom of Babylon. Having seceded from the Assyrian command, he set himself up as the new king of Babylonia. Later he entered into an alliance with Cyaxares I, king of the Medes. And that alliance was sealed by the king, giving his daughter, Princess Amuhia, in marriage to the young Prince Nebuchadnezzar.

A few years prior to his first attack on Judah, Nabopolassar laid siege to the city of Nineveh, one-time capital of Assyria. It fell before the armies of Babylon and Media in 612 B.C. This marked the end of Assyria's ruthless rule which for three centuries had terrorized surrounding nations.

Ashurbanipal's famous library was buried in the ruins, and lay undiscovered for almost 2,500 years, until Layard and others found it over a century ago. This ruin yielded a rich booty, especially the former library. Few other places have given so much aid to the science of archaeology.

The final collapse of the Assyrian kingdom left the whole area open. It was divided between Media and Babylonia. Cyaxares took all the northern section, while Nabopolassar laid claim to all the south, including Syria, Egypt, and Palestine. Judah, therefore, came under the jurisdiction of Babylon. Jehoiakim, king of Judah, was definitely pro-Egyptian, however, and foolishly felt that the nation's security depended upon Egypt rather than upon the living God. When Nebuchadnezzar besieged Jerusalem in 605 B.C., it was really to overthrow Egypt's influence in that area. Had Judah heeded the messages of the prophets, how different would have been the history of the Jews. The Scripture records that the Lord gave Jehoiakim into the hand of Nebuchadnezzar, who reduced Judah to the status of a vassal state.

God's Purpose Worked Out Through Babylon

International intrigues and rebellions were well known to young Daniel. When he and his royal companions were taken as hostages and made eunuchs in the service of the king of Babylon, it was no surprise but rather a fulfillment of Isaiah's prophecy uttered a hundred years earlier. Habakkuk, a decade or more earlier, had expressed his deep concern that the Lord seemed to be doing nothing to thwart the rising power of the Chaldeans. He reminded the Lord that spoiling and violence occurred everywhere and that wicked armies compassed the righteous. Habakkuk 1:2, 3. But the Lord said to him: "Behold . . . I will work a work in your days, which ye will not believe, though it be told you. For, lo, I raise up the Chaldeans, that bitter and hasty nation, which shall march through the breadth of the land, to possess the dwellingplaces that are not their's." Habakkuk 1:5, 6. The prophet could not understand this. He wondered why it was permitted. But the Lord said He had "ordained them for judgment" and "established them for correction." Habakkuk 1:12.

Habakkuk was shown that what was to happen was in the purpose of an all-wise God. He doubtless passed on this message to the young people in his classes; when Nebuchadnezzar arrived at the gates of Jerusalem, young Prince Daniel understood why. How greatly he prized the words of Isaiah, Micah, Habakkuk, Jeremiah, and the other prophets. If he did not actually have the writings, he knew the content of the prophets' messages.

Although exposed to the vice and corruption of an oriental court —and no other city was more vice-ridden than Babylon—Daniel maintained an unblemished life of practical holiness. And he lived a long life, extending from Nebuchadnezzar to Cyrus the Great. Jeremiah, Ezekiel, Ezra, and Zerubbabel, were all his contemporaries. We do not know the year of his death, but he was at least eighty-eight years old when he read the handwriting on the wall of the Babylonian palace the night of Belshazzar's feast. He witnessed the invasion of the Persian army, and was in his ninetieth year at least when thrown into the lions' den. He was honored with high office under Cyrus, king of Persia, and doubtless played an important role in influencing Cyrus to make the decree that permitted the Jews to return and rebuild the temple in Jerusalem. He may have watched the first caravan of rejoicing fellow countrymen as they left for the land of their fathers under the leadership of Zerubbabel and Joshua the high priest.

Daniel Through the Eyes of Contemporaries

Ezekiel mentions Daniel as an outstanding example of righteousness, coupling his name with Noah and Job. Ezekiel 14:14, 20. He also speaks of Daniel as a man of exceptional intelligence. Ezekiel 28:3.

Josephus, the Hebrew historian, refers to Daniel's skill in architecture. His book is written partly in Aramaic and partly in Hebrew, there being six chapters in each language. He may well have lived to be a hundred years old. Today the traveler to the acropolis of Susa (Shushan), one of the capitals of Elam (Daniel 8:2), is shown the supposed tomb of Daniel. While he was a great prophet, he did not come with a denunciation of specific sins and a plea for repentance as did others. But he did speak to his nation in an authoritative way. Never once did he use the regular formula, "Thus saith the Lord," for he spoke for God to a foreign court. He was statesman, prophet, and prime minister, first of Babylon and later of Medo-Persia.

We can learn wonderful lessons from this spiritual giant. His life spanned almost a century, and nothing in his long and active life reveals more clearly his character than when, as a youth of eighteen, he "purposed in his heart that he would not defile himself with the portion of the king's meat, nor with the wine which he drank." Daniel 1:8.

Eager to impress these brilliant young Judean captives and hasten their Chaldeanization, Nebuchadnezzar personally ordered their diet. This was, of course, part of a plan to change their life-style. To hasten this change the four were given idolatrous names. Daniel, which means "God is my Judge," was named Belteshazzar, "Bel protect his life"; Hananiah, "God is gracious," became Shadrach, "worship of the moon"; Mishael, "God has no equal," was given the name Meshach, "devotee of the moon god"; and Azariah was renamed Abednego "a servant of Nego or Nebo." For some reason Daniel's friends are subsequently known by these heathen names.

Royal Cuisine Refused

Sharing the bounties from the royal table was really a gracious act on the king's part. But these lads courteously refused it. They had been well trained at home and at school. To accept this provision would be to violate the food laws of Leviticus. Furthermore, they knew it was first offered to idols, perhaps to Marduk (Bel or Merodach) the chief god of Babylon. As spokesman for the group, Daniel requested Melzar, the chief steward, that they be given water instead of wine and "pulse" or vegetables in place of the king's meat. The Hebrew word *zero'im*, "pulse," is rendered "vegetables" or "grains" in other translations. In Isaiah 61:11 the word reads "things that are sown."

God brought Daniel into favor and tender love with the prince of the eunuchs. The tactful approach of Daniel is a wonderful example of godly humility and wisdom. "Prove thy servants ten days," he said. "Then let our countenances be looked upon before thee . . . : and as thou seest, deal with thy servants." It was actually a case of clinical nutrition. And it worked. Their countenances were fairer; they were well nourished and alert. But it was not only the radiance of good health; it was the outshining of God's presence. Their bodies were, indeed, the temples of the Holy Spirit.

God-given Knowledge and Skill

No wonder Melzar permitted them to continue their plain diet. What a demonstration of living a life of restraint and temperance rather than sensual indulgence! With what result? God gave these four young men "knowledge and skill in all learning and wisdom." Daniel 1:17. They underwent three years of study, and at the end of that time, when they stood before the king to be examined, Nebuchadnezzar, himself a trained Chaldean, "found them ten times better than *all* the magicians and astrologers that were in *all* his realm." Daniel 1:20.

At eighteen years of age Daniel was a man of leadership, a fact he early proved. Had he not taken the lead, one might never have heard of the other three. He possessed an "excellent spirit," and because of his integrity and unswerving loyalty he proved he could be trusted with the secrets of kings. He served as Nebuchadnezzar's

prime minister for perhaps forty years; when Babylon fell, he became prime minister of Medo-Persia. Daniel's strength was the
strength of righteousness. What man in all history can equal this
statesman-prophet in spiritual and political leadership?

2
Daniel at the Court
of Babylon

In the Old Testament nothing adverse is recorded against either Joseph or Daniel. Both of them were taken from their homes at the tender age of seventeen or eighteen, and neither ever saw his homeland again. Both endured hardships as slaves, yet both rose to become prime ministers of the empires in which they served.

Because these young men were destined for great leadership, God permitted hard experiences to help mold their characters. No one has better expressed the principles so essential in shaping great lives than has Angela Morgan:

When God Wants a Man

When God wants to drill a man
And thrill a man and skill a man;
When God wants to mold a man
To play the noblest part;
When He yearns with all His heart
To create so great and bold a man
That all the world shall praise—
Watch His method, watch His ways!
How He ruthlessly perfects
Whom He royally elects;
How He hammers him and hurts him
And with mighty blows converts him
Into trial shapes of clay which only God
　　　　　can understand—
While his tortured heart is crying and

he lifts beseeching hand!
How He bends, but never breaks,
When his good He undertakes—
How He uses whom He chooses
And with every purpose fuses him,
By every art induces him
To try his splendor out—
Yes, God knows what He's about.

When God wants to name a man
And fame a man and tame a man;
When God wants to shame a man
To do his heavenly best;
When He tries the highest test
That His reckoning may bring;
When He wants to make a king—

When the force that is divine
Leaps to challenge every failure and his
    ardor still is sweet
And love and hope are burning in the
    presence of defeat—

When the people need salvation
Doth he come to lead the nation.
Then to all God shows His plan
When the world has found—a man!
                    —Angela Morgan, adapted.

While Daniel served in positions of high service in a foreign land, he embodied truth and loyalty, adhered to principle, and was recognized even by his enemies as a master in statecraft.

1. He was of royal birth through the line of King Hezekiah. Daniel 1:3; 2 Kings 20:17, 18.
2. Neither money nor power could corrupt him. Daniel 5:17.
3. King Nebuchadnezzar recognized his brilliance as a scholar. Daniel 1:18, 20.
4. He permitted nothing to interfere with his regular periods of prayer. Daniel 6:10.

5. He carried on his heart the spiritual needs of his whole nation. Daniel 9:3, 17, 18.
6. Three times Gabriel bore witness that he was a man "greatly beloved." Daniel 9:23; 10:11, 19.
7. Even jealous enemies testified to his blameless character. Daniel 6:4, 5.
8. His courage and spiritual endowments were known to all. Daniel 5:22-28; 6:10.
9. Those closest to him recognized his "excellent spirit." Daniel 5:12; 6:3.
10. During his lifetime his righteousness and wisdom were proverbial. Ezekiel 14:20; 28:3.
11. Scripture ranks him with such stalwarts as Noah and Job. Ezekiel 14:19, 20.
12. While serving in the court, he personally wrote part of the book that bears his name. Daniel 7:1.
13. His messages influenced tremendously the later prophecies of Zechariah, Haggai, Paul, and John.
14. His prophecies were recognized as authentic by Jesus, the greatest teacher of all time. Matthew 24:15.
15. He was a student of "science" and a competent scholar when but a youth. Daniel 1:4, KJV and Moffatt.
16. He was made chief of the foremost group of scholars in Babylon. Daniel 2:48.

In this school of science were also astrologers, magicians, and philosophers. They were later known as the magi. The magician school continued for many centuries. The "wise men who came from the East" to Bethlehem were evidently students of nature and were led to worship the newborn King. "They belonged to a large influential class that included men of noble birth, . . . upright men who studied the indications of Providence in nature." *The Desire of Ages*, page 59.

While Daniel was promoted as overseer of the wise men, there is no intimation that he ever participated in the superstitious rites of the Chaldeans. Never did he compromise his faith in God. In *A Manual of the Ancient History of the East*, Lenormant describes this elite group of priests, astrologers, and Chaldeans as "the absolute governing class in politics. . . . At the head of this hierarchy and caste was Archi-Magus . . . ; he was, next to the king, the chief personage in the empire." Nebuchadnezzar elevated Daniel to this preeminent and authoratative position, as is made clear in Daniel 5:11.

Some readers may have the impression that Babylonian "wisdom" was little more than the pseudoscience of astrology and did not also include true astronomy. On this point George Stephen Goodspeed says of the Babylonians:

"The heavens were mapped out, and the courses of the heavenly bodies traced to determine the bearing of their movements upon human destinies. . . . The year of three hundred sixty-five and onefourth days was known, though the common year was reckoned according to twelve months of thirty days each, and equated with the solar year by intercalating a month at the proper times. Tables of stars and their movements, of eclipses of moon and sun, were carefully prepared. The year began with the month Nisan (March-April); the day with the rising of the sun; the month was divided into weeks of seven days; the day from sunrise to sunrise into twelve double hours of sixty minutes. The clepsydra [water clock] and the sun-dial were Babylonian inventions for measuring time."—
A History of the Babylonians and Assyrians, pages 93, 94.

Two outstanding Babylonian astronomers were Nabu-rimannus and Kidinnu. The former collected records covering two hundred years and compiled tables of the sun's motions in relation to the moon. He also calculated the daily revolutions of the earth and measured the length of the year as 365 days, 6 hours, 15 minutes, 41 seconds. Two thousand years later the telescope revealed that his measurement of the year was 26 minutes, 55 seconds too long. This splendid timetable is the earliest known recorded great constructive piece of astronomical science.

A little over a century later, Kidinnu made similar tables which have been proved even more accurate. It has been said that these scientists from about the time of David "are entitled to a place among the greatest astronomers. . . . They became the founders of astronomical science." Without a doubt some very remarkable scientific deductions were made in ancient Babylonia.

Morey, in his Ancient Peoples, says:

"As they discovered the regular movement of the heavenly bodies, they acquired some knowledge of astronomical science. They marked out the constellations and gave names to the stars. They divided the year into months, weeks, days, hours, minutes, and seconds. They measured the hours of the day by the sundial, and the hours of the night by the water clock. In their mathematics they adopted the decimal notation; but they also used another system of notation, that is, a system based on the number sixty— which we have inherited from them in our division of the hour and the minute into sixty parts. Besides acquiring considerable knowledge of mathematics, the Babylonians were the first to devise a regular system of weights and measures.

"The progress made by the early Babylonians in architecture, science, and the mechanic arts exercised a great influence upon later nations. Indeed, it would be difficult to overestimate the importance of these early steps in the world's civilization."—Pages 26, 27.

Daniel's Place Among the Scientists of His Day

As we noticed, Daniel headed this group of Chaldean "wise men." In fact, he remained chief counselor to King Nebuchadnezzar for about forty years. The king was himself a Chaldean—a scholar. That is why he was able to examine Daniel and his companions.

In Daniel, then, we see not only a great statesman recognized by both the Babylonian and Medo-Persian Empires but also a talented representative of the God who reveals secrets. With all the honors the world could give, however, he was also a humble servant of the Most High God. The messages he wrote and taught in his own generation were important, but those messages are even more vital to the present generation, for the things he foretold would happen in the "time of the end" are either in process of fulfillment now or will be in the very near future, for the end of all things is at hand.

Ezekiel's Estimate of Daniel

Ezekiel, a contemporary of Daniel, was another Jewish captive in Babylon. He belonged to the priestly line, while Daniel was of the royal line. Ezekiel, who was younger than Daniel, had the unusual opportunity to observe him at close range. Ezekiel was called of God to the office of both prophet and priest. He began his ministry some fourteen years after Daniel's arrival in Babylon, so at the time Ezekiel began to write Daniel was about forty years of age. At the time Ezekiel wrote of him, Daniel could have been close to fifty. Certain critics declare Daniel would have been too young to have earned such a reputation as we find recorded in Ezekiel 28:3. Writing of Lucifer, Ezekiel says, "Behold thou art wiser than Daniel; there is no secret that they can hide from thee." But as a chosen messenger of God, Daniel had plenty of time to demonstrate his wisdom and knowledge. Moreover he earned that reputation in a land that boasted greater wisdom than any previous generation. The Chaldean wise men, of which Daniel proved wiser than any, were recognized as the most famous and knowledgeable in the ancient world. We can well imagine what it meant to the Jewish captives, slaves, for the most part, to know of Daniel's presence in the highest councils of the empire. To know that at the head of the state and the "university" stood one of their own must have been wonderfully reassuring. He was their representative, their influential patron, loved by God and by the people.

As a priest (also a prophet) among the exiles, Ezekiel was probably settled in the community of Tel-abib on the canal Chebar, a short distance from the capital. Ezekiel 3:15. Delivering his divine warnings (verse 17), he too probably heard of what Daniel was doing at the administrative headquarters. And it was this younger messenger of God who linked the name of Daniel with the great righteous men of other days—Job and Noah. Ezekiel 14:14, 20. True Daniel was young when he became chief counselor to the king, but that was because he demonstrated so wonderfully his unusual God-given gifts when but twenty-one years of age. However, when Ezekiel wrote of him he had reached the zenith of his power and fame. Ezekiel may have had opportunity to see personally the evidence of Daniel's greatness and esteem.

Captive Jews Rebuild Babylon

The Jewish exiles played a great part in the rebuilding of the city of Babylon. It became the most ornate city of the ancient world, with its temples and palaces planned and inspired by Nebuchadnezzar. While he was their conqueror, he permitted the exiles to live in colonies of their own where they could carry out their religious customs. In fact, during these captivity years the synagogue came into being. There were no such places as synagogues before the Babylonian captivity. Ezekiel speaks of a "little sanctuary" which many believe has reference to the synagogue.

Jeremiah was not numbered among these exiles. He still lived in Jerusalem when he urged the exiles to build their own houses and serve their masters. Jeremiah 29:5-7. He foretold that they would remain in captivity for seventy years. Verse 10. Yet, while living in a foreign land they were still permitted to live as families. Daniel and his companions, however, had no such privilege.

Although living at the court, they, like the whole nation of Judah, were victims of God's judgment. But the judgments upon these young men were especially severe. The Scripture declares that Daniel and his three companions were princes, members of the royal family. They were born to rule and, as fathers of families, to guide their children in the ways of God. But instead they were destined to live as eunuchs in the service of their captors. When divine wrath is visited on a nation, the innocent suffer with the guilty. It has often been so.

More than a hundred years before Nebuchadnezzar came to power, Isaiah told King Hezekiah that because of his failure to represent the God of heaven rightly, when the ambassadors came to him from Babylon, his sons would be "eunuchs in the palace of the king of Babylon." Isaiah 39:7. And this is exactly what Daniel and his companions were—emasculated men with no hope of family or posterity. Think of what this meant to a genius like Daniel. Bred in the expectation of princely responsibility and sovereignty, he at last found himself destined to spend his life in the service of a heathen monarch in a foreign land!

The tragedy of Judah's national sin was compounded a thousand times as the parents were forced to see what happened to the flower of their youth. But with it all, these four young men, of whom Daniel was leader, remained noble examples of true knowledge and righteous living. By diligent study they prepared themselves for whatever places of trust they might be called to fulfill, and all four of them rose to positions of responsibility.

During Nebuchadnezzar's invasions of the Holy Land, Jeremiah was left in Jerusalem. He continued as the great prophetic figure to the nation already suffering divine judgments. On the other hand, Ezekiel prophesied to the exiles already in Babylon while Daniel served as prophet-statesman at this seat of political power. What a tremendous role he played in keeping the vision of the future clear to the captives! And not to them alone but also the Babylonians themselves, many of whom will no doubt inhabit the kingdom of glory because of Daniel's faithful witness.

Did Daniel write the book of Daniel? Jesus spoke of him as the "prophet." The Lord did not refer to him as a forger or a deceiver. Nor did He imply that some other person had written the book that bears Daniel's name.

In his book *Observations Upon the Prophecies of Daniel and the Apocalypse of St. John,* Sir Isaac Newton says: "Whoever rejects the prophecies of Daniel does as much as if he undermined the Christian religion, which so to speak, is founded on Daniel's prophecies of Christ."

Josephus, the noted Jewish historian, declared that the prophet-statesman himself wrote the book. In *Antiquities of the Jews,* 10:11: 7, he says: "All these things did this man leave in writing, as God had showed them to him, insomuch that such as read his prophecies, and see how they have been fulfilled, would wonder at the honour wherewith God honoured Daniel."

Daniel's Influence on Greek History

Josephus relates a moving incident in the life of Alexander which involved the book of Daniel. After telling how the nation was filled with fear when they heard that Alexander was making his way to Jerusalem, Josephus says: "Now Alexander, when he had taken Gaza, made haste to go up to Jerusalem; and Jaddua the high priest, when he heard that, was in an agony, and under terror, as not knowing how he should meet the Macedonians. . . . [But] God warned him in a dream . . . that he should take courage, and adorn the city, and open the gates; that the rest should appear in white garments, but that he and the priests should meet the king in the habits proper to their order, without the dread of any ill consequences, which the providence of God would prevent. . . . Alexander, when he saw the multitude at a distance, in white garments, while the priests stood clothed with fine linen, and the high priest in purple and scarlet clothing, with his mitre on his head, having the golden plate whereon the name of God was engraved, he approached by himself, and adored that name, and first saluted the high priest." In explanation of his act, he said, " 'I saw this very person in a dream, in this very habit, when I was at Dios in Macedonia. . . . [And] I believe that I bring this army under the Divine conduct, and shall therewith conquer Darius.' . . . And he came into the city. And when he went up into the temple, he offered sacrifice to God, according to the high priest's direction, and magnificently treated both the high priest and the priests. And when the Book of Daniel was shown him, wherein Daniel declared that one of the Greeks should destroy the empire of the Persians, he supposed that himself was the person intended."—*Antiquities of the Jews*, 11:8.

The prophecies of Daniel (chapters 7 and 8) so impressed Alexander, the Macedonian conqueror, that he became the protector of the Jews throughout his whole realm. And this occurred a century and a half before the date (165 B.C.) which Porphyry and the critics of our day assign to the writing of the book of Daniel!

While Daniel was writing his prophecies, he was prime minister of the empire that ruled the world and the acknowledged head of the Chaldean hierarchy, next to the king. Yet all the while he was carrying such tremendous responsibility as a statesman, he remained a loyal, dedicated messenger of the living God, one who, though exalted, did not forget his Hebrew companions.

"Then the king gave Daniel high honors and many great gifts, and made him ruler over the whole province of Babylon, and chief prefect over all the wise men of Babylon. Daniel made request of the king, and he appointed Shadrach, Meshach, and Abednego over the affairs of the province of Babylon; but Daniel remained at the king's court." Daniel 2:48, 49, RSV.

It has been truly said, "History follows the mold set for it by Daniel." The events of thousands of years have verified that his prophecies were truly of God.

3
Daniel in the Critics' Den

About two hundred years ago certain scholars of the rationalistic school attacked the book of Daniel. They said it is unreliable, both historically and prophetically. Because of a lack of correlative evidence concerning certain events recorded by Daniel, and also because of the prophet's predictions, they claimed the book could never have been written as prophecy, for no man knows the future. It must, therefore, have been written as history, and the writer, in order to gain prestige, used the name of Daniel.

The argument was not new. Porphyry, a neoplatonic philosopher and Greek historian born in Tyre in A.D. 233, had made the same claim.

Porphyry's Attack on Christianity

Enamored with the teachings of Plotinus, Porphyry gave himself to special study and later became a lecturer on philosophy in Rome. Defending polytheisim and the worship of the popular gods, he set himself to the task of destroying all that opposed it. Christianity, therefore, he violently attacked. He wrote on many subjects, but his best known works are fifteen books under the title, *Adversus Cristianos* (Against the Christians). Books 12 and 13 of this set are a bitter criticism of Daniel. And, strange as it may seem, his arguments still form the basis of theologians' attacks on Daniel.

His ideas were not accepted at all. This is evident from the fact that the Emperor Theodosius II ordered, in A.D. 435 and again in A.D. 448, Porphyry's books to be destroyed publicly. From that time until the rise of German Rationalism, around the middle of the eighteenth century, little was heard of this anti-Christian philosopher. However, when renewed attacks were made to discredit divine revelation—with claims that naturalism and reason are the only safe sources of knowledge—Porphyry's arguments were early picked up. In a few years his ideas echoed again in the classrooms. It was claimed, for example, that the book is really a forgery, a kind of religious novel, unreliable as history and impossible as prophecy. No man can foretell the future, declared Porphyry and his followers. Poor Porphyry! How little he and those who accepted his false teachings knew of the multiplied evidences that were to be unearthed in our day!

Theologians who deny the authenticity of the book of Daniel say that it must have been written about 165 B.C. during the Maccabean period. They assign it a place in the Jewish pseudepigrapha —a group of doubtful writings by unknown, uninspired authors, such as The Fourth Book of Ezra, The Testament of the Twelve Patriarchs, The Assumption of Moses, The Ascension of Isaiah, The Odes of Solomon, The Testament of Abraham, The Testament of Adam, and The Apocalypse of Baruch. The writers of these books used the names of Old Testament worthies in order to get their works accepted. They claimed to have visions and used apocalyptic symbols.

To place Daniel in this group reveals a pathetic ignorance of both the man and his message. Evidence in the book itself shows that the prophet Daniel wrote the book in the sixth century B.C. But "liberal" theology declares that it did not appear until the second century B.C., four hundred years later.

What is the purpose behind these claims? Certain critical scholars are desirous of stripping the Bible of everything supernatural or miraculous, leaving it merely a human production. To them the book of Daniel is the most vulnerable book of the sacred canon because it contains so much of the supernatural—so many visions, so many miracles, so many unusual happenings. These critical scholars, of course, rule out predictive prophecy.

We would not condemn all Biblical criticism. Much good has come as men have sought to understand the true history of the writers and their writings. In recent years we note with appreciation a new trend toward a reverent, believing approach rather than the virtual abandonment of the Sacred Scriptures. Every Bible-believing Christian can appreciate this. But in spite of these trends many scholars still cling to the claims of earlier writers. Many sincerely believe that the book of Daniel is a product of the second century B.C. rather than of the sixth.

The things which most challenged Porphyry some 250 years after Christ were the prophecies of Daniel. They were so accurate up to the time of his writing that he said they could not possibly have been written in advance. But what about all the centuries since? These, too, were foretold in Daniel's prophecies, some much more remarkable than those preceding Porphyry. In fact, prophecy is found in many books of the Word of God. Not only is prophecy predictive; it is also exhortative. While it unveils the future, it also leads men to live lives of justice and righteousness.

The Bible, a Book of Prophecy

Genuine prophecy is, however, unique to the Word of God. Other religions have their sacred books or scriptures; and, while some contain fine exhortations, none accurately foretells the future. If they did, their mistakes and guesses would soon reveal them to be spurious, for only the living God, the God of the Bible, knows the future. In fact, He stakes His deity on His ability to predict what is yet to happen. These words written by the prophet Isaiah, more than a hundred years before Daniel's day, set forth the claims of the living God: "Remember the former things of old: for I am God, and there is none else; I am God, and there is none like me, declaring the end from the beginning, and from ancient times the things that are not yet done, saying, My counsel shall stand, and I will do all my pleasure." Isaiah 46:9, 10. Again: "Who hath declared this from ancient time? who hath told it from that time? have not I the Lord? and there is no God else beside me; a just God and a Saviour." Isaiah 45:21. As we pursue our study of Daniel's book, we will see how clearly the Lord foretold the future.

When Daniel, the young Hebrew captive, stood before Nebuchadnezzar, he declared, "the great God hath made known to the king what shall come to pass hereafter." The Judeo-Christian religion is either a revealed religion recording the past and foretelling the future, or it is nothing at all. The ancient Hebrew prophets—

Daniel, Jeremiah, Moses, and Isaiah—possessed both insight and foresight. They were both forthtellers and foretellers. Peter says, "For the prophecy came not in old time by the will of man: but holy men of God spake as they were moved by the Holy Ghost." 2 Peter 1:21. Daniel was one of those "holy men" who spoke and wrote under the guidance of the Holy Spirit.

In that same letter the apostle Peter refers to his experience with James and John in the holy mount when Christ was transfigured before them. They saw His glory and heard the Father's voice declaring, "This is my beloved Son . . . ; hear ye him." But Peter says, "We have also a more sure word of prophecy; whereunto ye do well that ye take heed, as unto a light that shineth in a dark place." 2 Peter 1:19. What! More sure than what one sees and hears? Yes. The testimonies of the prophets are more sure than our senses. Yet, certain critics seem determined to destroy the prophetic element of the Bible.

Our Saviour proved His messianic ministry, not only by His miracles, but by the prophecies of the Old Testament. And in Gabriel's message to Daniel the very time when our Lord was to begin his miraculous ministry was clearly revealed. Moreover, Jesus knew it, for we read in Mark 1:14, 15, "Jesus came into Galilee, preaching the gospel of the kingdom of God, and saying, The time is fulfilled, and the kingdom of God is at hand." What time was fulfilled? The time specified in Daniel 9:25, 26. (This prophecy is the basis of chapter 12 of this book). In His first sermon in Nazareth after returning from His baptism by John, Jesus declared that He was fulfilling prophecy. Luke 4:21. Then, on the evening of His resurrection, having made a surprise entrance to the upper room where His disciples huddled together for fear of the Jews, the Saviour said, "These are the words which I spake unto you, when I was yet with you, that all things must be fulfilled, which were written in the law of Moses, and in the prophets, and in the psalms, concerning me." Luke 24:44.

Our Lord's first advent was foretold in marvelous detail in scores of prophecies. But Porphyry and the naturalistic critics of our time cannot accept prophecy as a possibility. So they reject the books of prophecy, such as Daniel and the Revelation, in the name of scholarship.

They reject Daniel not only because of the prophecies, but also because they allege that the history is unreliable. Let us examine just a few of the claims of these critics. The opening verses of Daniel speak of Nebuchadnezzar, king of Babylon, besieging Jerusalem in the reign of Jehoiakim. The critics used to say this is an error, for the event took place before Nebuchadnezzar's father, Nabopolassar, died. Therefore Nebuchadnezzar was not king of Babylon. But Jeremiah speaks of Nebuchadnezzar in the same way (Jeremiah 27:6). Daniel wrote his opening verses using his knowledge of current history at a time when Nebuchadnezzar *was* king.

Another criticism of Daniel's historic record concerns the spelling of the name Nebuchadnezzar. They say it should have been spelled Nebuchadrezzar, with an "r", as in Ezekiel. But Daniel spells it exactly as it is found in the books of Kings, Chronicles, Ezra, and Jeremiah. In fact, Jeremiah sometimes spells it as in Daniel and sometimes as in Ezekiel. A number of ancient history names in Scripture are spelled in varied forms. As an example, take the Syrian monarch mentioned in 2 Kings 15:29. There it is spelled Tiglath-pileser. But in 1 Chronicles 5:26 he is called Tilgath-pilneser. Other examples could be given. The critics themselves know that the transliteration of names from the Babylonian cuneiform into Hebrew or Aramaic sometimes varies. Literally, Nebuchadnezzar is Nabu-kudarri-ussar, meaning "Nabu protect the succession rights." In any case, the change from an "r" to an "n" is insignificant, giving no evidence for late authorship of Daniel's book as Porphyry claimed.

Archaeology Confirms Daniel's Record

The critics also question Daniel's use of the word "Chaldeans." Daniel speaks of them as astrologers and magicians, but critics have claimed that the word "Chaldean" referred to the nation of Babylon, not to a class of astrologers. Let us look at the facts. About a century after Daniel wrote, Herodotus visited Babylon, and he referred to the Chaldeans just as Daniel did. The critics must surely have overlooked Daniel's own words in chapter 5, verse 30, and chapter 9, verse 1, where he also refers to the king or the realm of the Chaldeans. Archaeological evidence shows the Chaldeans as a priestly caste, the elite of Babylon, and dedicated to the worship of the god Bel (Marduk). What we know of the Chaldeans today corroborates Daniel's description in detail.

As we noted before, part of Daniel's book was written in Hebrew and part in Aramaic. This fact gave critics another occasion to place its writing in the second century, alleging that the Aramaic of Daniel is late Palestinian, not sixth century. But the records of Qumran, recently discovered, contained scrolls written in Aramaic of the Maccabean period, at which time the critics declare Daniel was written. But the second century Aramaic in the scrolls is quite different from that of Daniel. Even more convincing are the Elephantine papyri, dated in the fifth century B.C., shortly after Daniel wrote. The Aramaic of these documents corresponds closely to Daniel's.

One of the critics' strongest points related to the four empires of Daniel's prophecies. Building on Porphyry's premise that Daniel is history, not prophecy, they claim that the succession of empires is not Babylon, Medo-Persia, Grecia, and Rome, but Babylon, Media, Persia, and Greece. Rome, they argue, had not become a world empire in his day, whereas Greece was the dominant power in the second century B.C. But they overlook the fact that Media and Persia were actually one empire when Babylon was overthrown. It was Medo-Persia that took the stage of world dominion in 539 B.C. The Medes joined the Persians in 550 B.C. and the two became a united empire years before they marched against Babylon. Medo-Persia was indeed the second of the world empires outlined in Daniel, chapters 2, 7, 8, and 11.

Belshazzar Emerges From Buried Cities

Daniel's mention of Belshazzar as the last king of Babylon has provided a major point of attack by the critics. Until recent years no other historical evidence confirmed the existence of a king named Belshazzar. This, they said, betrayed the ignorance of the writer and exposed the book as fiction. Ancient secular sources know to scholars indicated that Nabonidus, not Belshazzar, was the last king of Babylon. And Nabonidus was not killed; Cyrus captured him in Tema, northern Arabia. So Belshazzar was Exhibit A in the case against Daniel. But archaeologists have turned the tables. Today evidence shows not only that Belshazzar lived, but that he fulfilled the exact role recorded by Daniel. True, Nabonidus was his father, but from the third year of his reign, 553 B.C., Nabonidus shared the sovereignty with his elder son, Belshazzar, until the night he died at the hands of the Persians. See Daniel 5.

A crowning piece of evidence is a clay tablet bearing the names of both Nabonidus and Belshazzar as reigning kings.

Belshazzar's name in Babylonian cuneiform is Bel-shar-usur "Bel, protect the king." He was still a young man when he gathered his nobles for a blasphemous banquet. He had been a mere lad when he had witnessed Nebuchadnezzar's return to the throne after seven years of insanity.

During these years Nabonidus, later to become king, was an officer in the court of Babylon, so from his earliest years Belshazzar was accustomed to the throne and the protocol of royalty. When Belshazzar was 20 years old, Nabonidus, after some intrigue, ascended the throne and for the next seventeen years reigned as king of Babylon. For thirteen of those years he shared rulership with his son Belshazzar.

Just prior to the entry of the invading army, Daniel was brought in to read the letters of fire, so boldly traced on the wall, that told the doom of the kingdom. The wise men, the astrologers, the Chaldeans, together with the soothsayers or spiritualists, were unable to interpret the writing. When God's prophet appeared, the king told him that if he could interpret the message he would be made "the third ruler in the kingdom." Why not the second ruler? The answer is simple. Belshazzar himself was already the second, as coruler with his father Nabonidus.

Yes, the evidence concerning Belshazzar is so convincing today that no well-informed student of Babylonian history would doubt either his existence or his kingship. He was, in truth, the last king at Babylon, his father having gone to Tema at an earlier time.

Cyrus moved with his army toward the seat of the empire and overran the kingdom. The events of his conquest were recorded on the Nabunaid Chronicle. We should note in passing that when a heavenly messenger wrote on the palace wall, the interpretation said that the "kingdom is given to the Medes and Persians," not to the Medes alone as the critics claim. We have already noted the attempt to make Media the second of the four successive empires outlined by Daniel. But history shows that the Persians were united with the Medes in their conquest. In fact, the Persians were the stronger of the two kingdoms. This was clearly indicated in chapter 7 in the symbol of the bear which raised itself up on one side. Also, in chapter 8 we have the symbol of the ram with two horns, one higher than the other. If, as the critics claim, Persia was the third empire in the succession, how could it have been represented in chapter 7 by a leopard with four heads or in chapter 8 by a goat with four horns? Was Persia ever so divided? Strange the lengths to which men will go in their efforts to prove that Daniel did not write prophecy but only recorded history under the guise of prophecy.

Dr. E. B. Pusey, in the introduction to his work, *Lectures on Daniel the Prophet*, says: "The book of Daniel is especially fitted to be a battle field in faith and unbelief. It admits of no half-measures. It is either Divine or an imposture." The tragedy is that the assailants, the critics, are usually not avowed enemies of Christianity but often professors in seminaries who train the preachers of tomorrow.

Four Challenging Questions

It is tragic how far some critics will go in the name of scholarship until every prophecy, every miracle, and almost every historic event recorded in the book of Daniel is either ridiculed or ripped from the record. We would like to ask four questions which demand clear answers:

(1) If the book of Daniel was a forgery, how did it get into the Old Testament canon? References from the books of the Maccabees (c. 165 B.C.) indicate that Daniel was then a part of the canon of Scripture. See 1 Maccabees 2:51-60; cf Daniel 1:7; 3:26; 6:23.

(2) If the book of Daniel was not written until 165 B.C., how was it ever included in the Septuagint? This great translation has been assigned by some to the third century B.C., long before 165 B.C., the date some scholars ascribe to Daniel.

(3) Why do the critics say Daniel's reference to the doctrine of the resurrection dates the writing? According to their claim, this doctrine was not known in the sixth century. Yet, one of the clearest statements in Scripture concerning the resurrection is found in Job 19:25, 26, possibly the oldest book in the Bible. Then what

about Isaiah 26:19? "Thy dead men shall live, together with my dead body shall they arise." Isaiah wrote at least 150 years before Daniel.

(4) Who was the man of genius who penned this book foretelling the future of our planet and declaring the year the Messiah would begin His ministry? Daniel also predicted the scattering of the Jews by the Romans and the apostasy of a great anti-Christian power of later centuries. If this was not Daniel, then who was it?

In the days of the Maccabees, when the critics say the book was written, the people lamented that there was no prophet in the land, and that there was great tribulation in Israel, and "no prophet appeared." 1 Maccabees 9:27. Yet, critics say this book of Daniel appeared to be written in 165 B.C.! We ask, Who wrote it? An "unknown, pious Jew" writing in the days of Antiochus Epiphanes?

W. A. Criswell has stated it well: "They [the critics] cannot hold up their heads in the white light of the historic past."

And Joseph P. Free gives this lucid statement: "There is no first-rate liberal today, as far as the writer knows, who urges the old objection concerning Belshazzar. . . .

"The detailed facts are that Nabonidus, in one sense the last king of Babylon, was not killed by the invading Persians, but was given a pension by his conquerors. On the other hand, Belshazzar, elevated to the position of ruler of Babylon by his father, was killed when the city of Babylon was taken, as indicated in Daniel 5:20. The matter concerning Belshazzar, far from being an error in the Scriptures, is one of the many striking confirmations of the Word of God which have been demonstrated by archaeology."—*Archaeology and Bible History*, page 235.

When Daniel served as prime minister of Medo-Persia after Babylon's fall, the critics of his day had him thrown into the lions' den in order to get rid of him. He was, at that time, about ninety years old. Can we imagine what it would be like to spend the night with great hungry cats? The next morning, when the king asked: "Is thy God . . . able to deliver thee from the lions?" Daniel answered with assurance: "My God hath sent his angel, and hath shut the lions' mouths, that they have not hurt me."

The same God who shut the mouths of those savage beasts and spared the life of His prophet lives still, and in many ways He exposes the crumbling foundation upon which the critics' arguments rest. He who delivered His faithful servant long ago is again delivering Daniel from his "enemies" as archaeology and history confirm the accuracy of his writings. The stones of a hundred buried cities shout in the ears of an unbelieving world, "God's Word is truth!" All the critics put together, from Porphyry's time until now, could never produce one chapter of Daniel's book. God gave him the visions and then guided his mind as he wrote the prophecies.

4
Prophetic Panorama
of History to Be

As we begin the study of the second chapter of Daniel, let us note again the first verse of chapter 1. "The Lord *gave* Jehoiakim king of Judah into his [Nebuchadnezzar's] hand." Why did Israel's God make such a gift? Obviously to punish His people for their continued blasphemous iniquity. But there was an even deeper purpose. God delivered Israel from Egyptian slavery and placed them in Canaan that they might be His light bearers to the world. "I have endowed him with my spirit," said Jehovah, "to carry true religion to the nations." Isaiah 42:1, Moffatt. But Israel never measured up to that responsibility. Instead, they hedged themselves about in the Land of Promise, caring little about the surrounding nations who, in their darkness and superstition, continued their idolatrous worship.

Israel's Failure to Fulfill God's Purpose

When Israel failed to carry out its God-given responsibility, the Lord permitted a heathen monarch to invade Jerusalem and take His people captive. Seeing the finest of Judah's youth, such as Daniel and his companions, wrenched from their homes and taken as slaves into Babylon was a terrible shock to the Jews. Doubtless many asked if God had forgotten His promise. No, He had not forgotten, but He had to adapt His plan so as to carry out His original purpose. An all-seeing providence has through the centuries been at work permitting the rise and fall of nations and even the overthrow of His own people as a nation. "In the annals of human history, the growth of nations, the rise and fall of empires, appear as if dependent on the will and prowess of man; the shaping of events seems, to a great degree, to be determined by his power, ambition, or caprice. But in the word of God the curtain is drawn aside, and we behold, above, behind, and through all the play and counterplay of human interest and power and passions, the agencies of the All-merciful One, silently, patiently working out the counsels of His own will."—Ellen G. White, *Prophets and Kings*, pages 499, 500.

In no other portion of the Bible are these principles more profoundly portrayed than in the second chapter of Daniel. There the whole sweep of history from Daniel's day to our own time and beyond is clearly presented. This fascinating story focuses on a confrontation between two young men—one a slave, the other a king. And this confrontation came about in a strange but simple way. The king had a dream; not an unusual thing, especially in that land where the meaning of dreams meant so much. But the impression on the mind of this monarch was profound, so much so that he determined to know its meaning.

Failure of Babylon's Wise Men

A whole retinue of "wise men"—astrologers, magicians, spirit mediums, clairvoyants—peopled the court of Babylon. The king employed them for the very purpose of unraveling mysteries. Sure, they insisted that they could tell Nebuchadnezzar the meaning of his dream. But there was one big problem—the king had forgotten the dream, although he was sure it was important. The God of heaven had made his mind a blank to the details of the dream in order that these so-called "wise men" could not give Nebuchadnezzar a false interpretation.

When the frustrated king summoned his counselors, these educators, these mind readers, these stargazers, all failed. They assured him, however, that if he told them what he had seen they would be able to give the interpretation. The more these men hedged, the more impatient the king became. But they continued to tell him that his demand was not only unreasonable but impossible. Only "the gods, whose dwelling is not with flesh" could give him the answer. In that they were right. But their failure infuriated the king, who charged them with speaking "lying and corrupt words." The limitations of these palace aides had become all too evident. In his rage the king blurted out, in essence, "There is only one end for all of you. I will have you destroyed." It was a brutal decision, but in keeping with the practice of ancient dictators. So the executioners made ready to carry out the order. The record says, "it was urgent."

Daniel and his companions, as comparatively recent arrivals, were evidently not consulted, but they were numbered among the Babylonian wise men. When the executioners came to inform Daniel of the situation, he asked, "Why is the decree so hasty from the king?" He then requested an audience with the monarch. Daniel promised that if given time he would tell the dream and also the interpretation. Thus he staked his life upon God's promise to hear his prayer. Failure to keep his word would, he knew, bring terrible retribution. He told the king he had not the slightest notion concerning the dream, but he knew Someone who did know. He had faith. His request was granted.

And what did Daniel do? He called his companions, and together they laid the matter before the living God—One who never fails to honor those who put their trust in Him. They spent the night in prayer, and during the silent watches the Lord revealed the dream to Daniel in a vision. He also gave him its meaning and its message.

Before sharing it with the king, Daniel remembered to thank God: "Blessed be the name of God for ever and ever: for wisdom and might are his: and he changeth the times and the seasons: he removeth kings, and setteth up kings: he giveth wisdom unto the wise, and knowledge to them that know understanding: he revealeth the deep and secret things: he knoweth what is in the darkness, and the light dwelleth with him. I thank thee, and praise thee, O thou God of my fathers, who hast given me wisdom and might, and hast made known unto me now what we desired of thee: for thou hast now made known unto us the king's matter."

Some have seen in Daniel's prayer the influence of Habakkuk's revelation of God. Godly teachers can leave lasting impressions on young men. Fellowship and communion in prayer is one of life's richest experiences. When the apostles of the New Testament came together and prayed, the very walls of the building were shaken. True prayer can be the greatest power known to man. Daniel could have prayed alone, but he sought the companionship of his friends. There is great power in prayer fellowship.

Daniel Meets the King's Demand

The next day, instead of being brought before the executioners, Daniel stands before the king. Erect in the presence of royalty, he unfolds the message that changes the whole atmosphere. Without the slightest indication of boasting, Daniel tells God's message to the ruthless ruler of much of the then-known world.

"Art thou able to make known to me the dream," asks Nebuchadnezzar, "and the interpretation?"

Quickly turning the question from himself to his Lord, Daniel reminds the king that the astrologers, the magicians, even the whole retinue of soothsayers have been unable to meet his demand. "But," Daniel declares, "there is a God in heaven that revealeth secrets, and maketh known to the king Nebuchadnezzar what shall be in the latter days." Daniel 2:28. He also makes clear to the king that "this secret is not revealed to me for any wisdom that I have more than any living." Then young Daniel focuses the monarch's mind on the God of heaven, but before revealing the dream he has one request: "destroy not the wise men of Babylon."

Nothing more completely reveals the character of Daniel. As did the Saviour he represented, he prays for those who do not worship the true God. The wise men naturally were jealous of Daniel's wisdom, for Nebuchadnezzar had already pronounced him and his companions "ten times better" in matters of wisdom and understanding "than all the magicians and astrologers that were in all his realm." Daniel 1:20.

Picture the king listening spellbound to this 21-year-old wise man, who says, "Thou, O king, sawest, and behold a great image," a mighty colossus, "whose brightness was excellent, . . . and the form thereof was terrible. This image's head was of fine gold, his breast and his arms of silver, his belly and his thighs of brass, his legs of iron, his feet part of iron and part of clay." Then he tells the king, "While you looked, a stone was hewn from the mountain, not by human hands; it struck the image on its feet of iron and clay and shattered them." Daniel 2:34, NEB. And the king's memory reconstructs the scene as this mighty metal-and-mud man crumbles to pieces; he sees the shattered remains swept away by a strong wind, leaving the place as clean as a summer threshing floor.

The King Listens Spellbound

But this is not all. "The stone that smote the image became a great mountain, and filled the whole earth." Daniel 2:35. We can almost hear the king saying to himself: "Yes, that is exactly what I saw. Nothing added. Nothing left out. But does it have any meaning?"

Yes, it certainly has meaning, not only for Nebuchadnezzar but for every ruler and every person down to the end of time. Entranced, the king listens as Daniel continues. "This is the dream; and we will tell the interpretation thereof." The young prophet tactfully tells the king that his empire came into being not because of the strength of his well-trained armies, but because it was all in the purpose of God. "Thou . . . art a king of kings," he says, "for the God of heaven hath given thee a kingdom, power, and strength, and glory." In other words, yours is a given power, a given glory, and "wheresoever . . . men dwell, the beasts of the field and the fowls of the heaven hath he given into thine hand, and hath made thee ruler over them all. *Thou art this head of gold.*"

A smile of satisfaction is seen on the king's countenance, but Daniel continues. "After thee shall arise another kingdom inferior to thee"—not greater, but inferior—"and another third kingdom of brass, which shall bear rule over all the earth."

Before Nebuchadnezzar fell asleep on the night of his dream, he had been pondering the future. He wondered what would happen to his expanding empire after he died. "As you lay in bed," said Daniel, "came thoughts of what would be hereafter, and he who reveals mysteries made known to you what is to be." Daniel 2:29, RSV. There will be other empires, Daniel stated; in fact three others—no more, no less. And each succeeding empire will be inferior to the one before; inferior in concentrated wealth, but superior in strength and territory. Then, as the image stood in all its glory, suddenly a stone struck the colossus on the feet—not the head, but the feet—and the whole thing crumbled to pieces. Then a great wind came and carried everything away; not a fragment was left. But the stone that smote it began to grow until it filled the whole earth. "The God of heaven [will] set up a kingdom," said Daniel; and that kingdom of glory "shall not be left to other people, . . .

and it shall stand for ever." And the youthful prophet concluded his exposition with the emphatic declaration: "The dream is certain, and the interpretation thereof sure."

No wonder the king was troubled. No wonder he wanted someone to give the meaning. Was it a nightmare or a revelation? He did not know. What Nebuchadnezzar needed was "an interpreter, one among a thousand" (Job 33:23), and Daniel proved to be such an interpreter. This mighty colossus in the form of a man was actually a forecast of man's attempt to govern himself apart from God.

"The Times of the Gentiles"

When Israel was delivered from Egypt and was established as a nation at the crossroads of the world, God designed that they should teach the nations true religion. Instead, Israel followed the world into idolatry. Instead, the world led them into corrupting ways of witchcraft. So the Lord permitted Nebuchadnezzar to invade their land, to destroy their city, and to overthrow the throne of Judah. That was the beginning of Gentile rulership. Because of Israel's failure, the Lord may well have permitted the overthrow of Jerusalem in order to teach His people to depend on the living God for their protection and not on alliances with the world. Israel, instead of taking its place as the head of nations as God intended, now found herself in the hands of Gentile powers.

God's original purpose for Jerusalem was that it would stand as a great administrative center, an example to the world. Had His people obeyed Him, the city of Jerusalem would have stood forever. Jeremiah 17:25. But the nation failed to live up to her high destiny, and this led the great prophet to mourn that "the sin of Judah is written with a pen of iron . . . : it is graven upon the table of their heart." Verse 1. As a last appeal, Jeremiah was told to stand by the gate where the kings of Judah come in and out and deliver this message: "Thus saith the Lord; Take heed to yourselves, and bear no burden on the sabbath day, nor bring it in by the gates of Jerusalem; . . . neither do ye any work, but hallow ye the sabbath day, as I commanded your fathers. . . . Then there shall enter into the gates of this city kings and princes sitting upon the throne of David . . . : and this city shall remain for ever." Jeremiah 17:21, 22, 25.

What was their response? "They obeyed not, . . . but made their neck stiff, that they might not hear, nor receive instruction." Verse 23. The time came when "there was no remedy." See 2 Chronicles 36:14-17. True to the prophecy, the city was invaded and overthrown. Since then the Jews have never had a king or a throne. For 1,900 years they have been a scattered people among the nations while Gentile nations have led and ruled the world. This will continue until the coming of the King of kings, who will reign forever.

Babylon Gathers Wealth of the Nations

The sweep of history was outlined before Nebuchadnezzar and emphasized by the contrasting metals of the image. Now let us note the significance of these successive empires. The head of gold pictured Babylon. Under Nebuchadnezzar Babylon was the recognized center of wealth and glory. Gold flowed into it from all the provinces of the empire. The immense treasures gathered by king Solomon and brought to Jerusalem were later confiscated and carried to Babylon. Tremendous quantities of gold and bronze made Babylon the wealthiest city of its time.

When Herodotus, the ancient historian, visited Babylon a century after Nebuchadnezzar's day, he found an abundance of gold still there. Temples, altars, shrines—all were plated with this precious metal. Jeremiah says, "Babylon hath been a golden cup in the Lord's hand." Jeremiah 51:7. Isaiah spoke of Babylon as "the glory of kingdoms, the beauty of the Chaldees' excellency." Isaiah 13:19.

The Babylon of Nebuchadnezzar was not this city's beginning. It was probably the first city built after the Flood. Genesis 10:10. It flourished for hundreds of years. But after the reign of Hammurabi, king of ancient Babylon, it declined until it was little more than a wayside town. Sennacherib of Assyria thoroughly destroyed the ancient city in 689 B.C., but Nabopolassar, father of Nebuchadnezzar, rebuilt it, again making it a great center of trade and industry.

In his book The Bible as History, Dr. Werner Keller says that "its ancient power and glory had no equal in the ancient world." —Page 289. Not only was the city the center of wealth and industry but also the center of religion. The name "Babylon" came from the word *Babili,* meaning "gate of the gods." It was first built by Nimrod, who founded the Babylonian mystery religion at the time of the building of the Tower of Babel. The Scriptures speak of Nimrod as "a mighty hunter." He was not only politically powerful but a rebel against heaven. The name Nimrod means "he shall rebel." *The Jewish Encyclopedia* tells that Nimrod was "he who made all the people rebellious against God." He was the priest-king of devil worship, and Babylon became the headquarters of the mystery cults, a counterreligion.

The antithesis of all this was Jerusalem which means "city of peace." This makes all the more remarkable the statement of Daniel 1:2: "The Lord *gave* Jehoiakim king of Judah into his hand." God designed this disciplinary action on His part to teach Israel lessons they could learn no other way. Even when the seventy years of the Jews' Babylonian exile ceased and they returned to their homeland, Jerusalem failed to regain the greatness it had formerly enjoyed.

Babylon's glory was also short-lived. After only seventy years it passed into the hands of the Persian conqueror. The last king of Babylon was slain in the midst of a royal banquet.

Medo-Persia Moves Into World Leadership

Those words "after thee shall arise another kingdom inferior to thee" must have sounded strange to the king, for usually the superior conquers the inferior. But just as silver is inferior to gold in value, so the next universal kingdom, Medo-Persia, was inferior to Babylon in wealth and luxury. What Daniel actually said in Aramaic was, "After thee shall arise another kingdom downward from thee, earthward from thee." It would be downward in quality but earthward in extent, occupying more land surface.

Persia, however, was known for her treasures of silver. Xerxes, a prominent king of Persia, inherited immense hoards of silver from his father, Darius Hystaspes. In Hebrew, as in all Semitic languages, the word for money, *keseph,* is the same as is used for silver. In the Medo-Persian Empire reputedly all taxes had to be paid in silver. Consequently, the kings of this second empire grew extremely wealthy in silver. The empire lasted about 200 years, from 539 to 332 B.C.

Then came a third kingdom of brass, or bronze. (The "brass" of the KJV should be "bronze.") This was the Grecian Empire, which by a rapid series of conquests, replaced Medo-Persia. The thighs and abdomen of the image were of this material—a forecast of the "brazen coated Greeks" as they were called. This was the third Gentile power to "bear rule over all the earth." Daniel 2:39. The Greeks were experts in the molding of bronze. The soldiers wore breastplates of bronze, helmets of bronze, and carried shields of bronze. They carried bronze swords.

Alexander Builds the Grecian Empire

Alexander the Great, son of King Philip of Macedon, showed signs of genius even when a teen-ager. His father procured for him the best possible tutor, the great philosopher Aristotle. Alexander kept in close touch with his teacher throughout all his military campaigns. By the time he was twenty-five he had the world at his feet, but he never really conquered himself.

Returning with his troops from India, he reached Babylon, intending to make that city his world capital. His men were active in a great building program when one of his favorite generals died. This so grieved Alexander that it is said he drank the intoxicating "cup of Hercules." This brought on a very high fever, and he died in his wife's arms in 332 B.C. He conquered the world in eight short years but slipped into silence at the age of thirty-three.

Realizing that their leader had only hours to live, his generals asked, "To whom will you give the kingdom?"

"To the strongest," he replied.

The leading generals tested their strength against each other. "So Alexander . . . died. And his servants bore rule every one in his place. And after his death they all put crowns upon themselves. So did their sons after them many many years; and evils were multiplied in the earth." 1 Maccabees 1:7-9. The Grecian Empire was plunged into a state of turmoil and civil war, lasting about three decades. The kingdom finally disintegrated and later succumbed to the armies of the emerging power of Rome.

Rome Rules the World

The Battle of Pydna, June 22, 168 B.C. marks the time when Alexander's homeland fell before the Romans. Thus the empire of

Alexander which had already begun to crumble before Roman pressure, was whittled down piece by piece until Rome ruled the Mediterranean world and beyond to Britain in the north.

"The fourth kingdom shall be strong as iron: forasmuch as iron breaketh in pieces and subdueth all things: and as iron that breaketh all these, shall it break in pieces and bruise." Daniel 2:40.

For more than 500 years Rome seemed almost unconquerable. Her standards waved from the British Isles to the Arabian Gulf, from the North Sea to the Sahara Desert, from the Atlantic to the Euphrates. Her Ceasars were worshipped as gods, and by her invincible will she made every country under her influence a prison house for those who disagreed. The historian Edward Gibbon says, "To resist was fatal, and it was impossible to fly."—*The Decline and Fall of the Roman Empire*, Vol. 1, p. 190.

"Three fifths of the population of the city of Rome were slaves," says Schlegel, in his *Philosophy of History*, page 261. They were just chattels with a voice. It was as if the iron-shod god of war actually bestrode the globe; with every step new currents of blood poured forth. It was a regime of force and brute strength, but God can cause "the wrath of man" to praise him. Psalm 76:10. So in spite of man's roughshod cruelty, God was working out His plan.

Roman Roads Aid Christianity

While the Greeks carried their language throughout the Near and Middle East in preparation for the spread of the gospel, Rome built roads from Palestine to Britain, making travel possible for the messengers of Christianity. Her enforcement of law, with her expensive postal system, also aided the carrying of the news of salvation. Her *Pax Romana*, with two centuries of relative stability in the Mediterranean world, facilitated Christian evangelism. Paul wrote that the message of Jesus had reached "every creature which is under heaven." Colossians 1:23.

The iron element in the metal image was not to last forever. It stood on feet of clay with a mixture of iron. Daniel emphasized the feet and toes, stating that the fourth empire would not be overthrown by another universal empire but would be replaced by a collection of smaller nations warring among themselves. How accurately history fulfills prophecy!

Empire Divided Into Ten Parts

"The iron monarchy of Rome," to use Gibbon's expression, was broken into fragments by barbarian tribes, so that by A.D. 476 the strong empire was broken and Western Europe was divided into ten parts. These were the Lombards, the Alemanni, the Anglo-Saxons, the Ostrogoths, the Burgundians, the Franks, the Suevi, the Vandals, the Visigoths, and the Heruli. These were actually the progenitors of the nations of modern Europe—some strong, others weak, as indicated by the mixture of iron and clay. But the most important feature of this strange combination was their inability to adhere or unite. During fifteen centuries, strong dictators have tried to weld them and build a facsimile of the old Roman Empire. While they at times neared their goal, they always failed. Think of Charlemagne, Charles V, Louis XIV, Napoleon, Kaiser William II, Adolph Hitler—all of whom tried and failed. Something mysterious seemed to block the way. Seven words of prophecy stood between them and success. The Scripture says, "They shall not cleave one to another." Treaties, peace pacts, agreements of all kinds have been signed, sealed—and broken. As many as 4,568 treaties and international agreements were submitted before the old League of Nations between May 10, 1920 and May 19, 1939. But the treaties did not prevent World War II.

Attempts to Avert War

Daniel said to the astonished king: "As you saw the iron mixed, so shall they be mixed in marriage, but they will not hold together, just as iron does not mix with clay." Daniel 2:43, Berkeley Revised. Before the global war of 1914-1918 most European monarchs were related by marriage; but that, too, proved an ineffectual amalgam. The alliances based on marriage bonds dissolved in the crucible of war.

Today we witness another attempt to weld fragmented Europe, the nations that once formed the Roman Empire. We refer to the Common Market, which aims to unify their monetary systems, weights and measures, and military equipment, and establish a central government similar to the Federal Government of the United States of America. Robert Margolin says, "The sweeping changes together with the standardizing of the antitrust laws, transport rates, wage levels, and business and consumer taxes will lead almost imperceptibly to a politically united Europe."

It is significant that some of the outstanding statesmen who brought the Common Market to fruition were prominent Roman Catholic laymen: Paul Henri Spaak of Belgium, and Konrad Adenauer of West Germany. At the same time the patriarch of Venice, Cardinal Ulbani, urged that "all Italian Catholics give it their full support." The objective of this effort was a united Europe

A newspaper release by J. Opie of Rome appeared on April 2, 1962. Under the title, "Vatican Hails Common Market," it said: "The Vatican, usually cautious over political changes of its own, now considers the Common Market the work of divine Providence.

"Not since the times of Spain's Charles V has a Roman Catholic force been so strongly willed. Not since the end of the Holy Roman Empire has the Holy See been offered a Roman Catholic rallying point like the Common Market. If the 'Pact of Rome' which created the Common Market had been signed within the Vatican walls, it could not have favored the church more."

This writer then emphasizes that, of the 175 million population in the original six countries, more than 134 million are Roman Catholics. He concludes: "Small wonder then that the Roman Catholic Church is smiling benignly over the formation of what one Vatican official defined as 'the greatest Catholic superstate the world has ever known! The Holy See has now set aside one day in the year in honor of the 'Madonna of the Common Market,' when prayers are said and candles are lit in all the churches for the intervention of the Virgin Mary in what is, after all, the greatest Roman Catholic business deal in history."

To the student of Bible prophecy this statement from a Roman Catholic source must be impressive. When the Roman Empire broke up into fragmentary kingdoms, The Holy See soon saw an unusual opportunity to exercise political control. Through the Holy Roman Empire, a totally artificial conglomerate, and by interference in other national governments the papacy dominated European affairs for more than a thousand years. However, the Protestant Reformation in the sixteenth century and weaknesses within the church began to erode papal control. So, when General Berthier of Napoleon's army took Pope Pius VI prisoner in 1798, the era of Rome's political supremacy came to an end. As John the revelator foretold, this religio-political power received a "deadly wound," or "death-stroke." But the same verse also said that the wound would be healed and then all the world would wonder with great admiration. Revelation 13:3. We now see the recovery of that power; one method might well be the Common Market. It was Napoleon who said, "There will be no repose in Europe until it is under one Emperor whose officers would be kings."

Napoleon actually planned to bring this about. But as H. M. S. Richards has said: "He was smashing his fists against God's prophecy. 'They shall not cleave one to another.' "—*One World,* page 179. Napoleon met his Waterloo and died in exile a crushed and defeated man as were all the others who tried.

When this great prophetic outline was first interpreted to Nebuchadnezzar, he was looking into the future, scarcely any of which had been fulfilled. But today we look back over 2,500 years and see each segment of the prophecy remarkably fulfilled. How accurately history has met the prophetic forecast! All that is left is the last great event—the ushering in of the eternal kingdom of glory. Our next chapter unfolds the climactic events which will bring an end to human history and usher in the promised new heaven and new earth where disease and death, lawlessness and war, will never be known. Would you be ready if that kingdom were to come today? Right now you can be quietly accepting Jesus Christ as your Saviour and coming King.

5
The Mystic
Stone Kingdom

How impressive are the words of Daniel, the Hebrew captive, to the young king, Nebuchadnezzar.

" 'As you looked, a stone was cut out by no human hand, and it smote the image on its feet of iron and clay, and broke them in pieces; then the iron, the clay, the bronze, the silver, and the gold, all together were broken in pieces, and became like the chaff of the summer threshing floors; and the wind carried them away, so that not a trace of them could be found. But the stone that struck the image became a great mountain and filled the whole earth.

" 'This is the dream; now we will tell the king its interpretation. You, O king, the king of kings, to whom the God of heaven has given the kingdom, the power, and the might, and the glory, and into whose hand he has given, wherever they dwell, the sons of men, the beasts of the field, and the birds of the air, making you rule over them all—you are the head of gold. After you shall arise another kingdom inferior to you, and yet a third kingdom of bronze, which shall rule over all the earth. And there shall be a fourth kingdom, strong as iron, because iron breaks to pieces and shatters all things; and like the iron which crushes, it shall break and crush all these. And as you saw the feet and toes partly of potter's clay and partly of iron, it shall be a divided kingdom; but some of the firmness of iron shall be in it, just as you saw iron mixed with the miry clay. And as the toes of the feet were partly iron and partly clay, so the kingdom shall be partly strong and partly brittle. As you saw the iron mixed with miry clay, so they will mix with one another in marriage, but they will not hold together, just as iron does not mix with clay. And in the days of those kings the God of heaven will set up a kingdom which shall never be destroyed, nor shall its sovereignty be left to another people It shall break in pieces all these kingdoms and bring them to an end, and it shall stand forever; just as you saw that a stone was cut from a mountain by no human hand, and that it broke in pieces the iron, the bronze, the clay, the silver, and the gold. A great God has made known to the king what shall be hereafter. *The dream is certain, and its interpretation sure.'*" Daniel 2:34-45, RSV.

Imagine the thoughts that must have surged through the mind of Nebuchadnezzar as Daniel came to the climax of his interpretation—"after thee . . . another kingdom" and "another third kingdom" until the mighty monarchy of Rome appears. But even that great empire was not to last. Just as the prophecy indicated, it broke up as the barbaric invasions divided Europe into ten major fragments.

Then the king saw a stone coming from somewhere and smashing against the feet of clay and iron. Afterward the whole thing crumbled to pieces, and a hurricane carried it away. Strangest of all, the stone that struck the image "became a great mountain, and filled the whole earth."

What can it all mean? What is the stone cut out of the mountain without hands which grew until it filled the whole earth? The coming universal kingdom will not be founded by ingenious men but by the mighty God. It is called the stone kingdom, and the Scriptures have much to say about this stone. When Jacob, in God's name, blessed his son Joseph he said, "His bow abode in strength, and the arms of his hands were made strong by the hands of the mighty God of Jacob; (from thence is the shepherd, the stone of Israel)." Genesis 49:24.

Here the stone is linked with the Shepherd of Israel. And when our Lord answered a question put to Him by the chief priests and scribes, He quoted Psalm 118:22, 23, saying: "What is this then that is written, The stone which the builders rejected, the same is become the head of the corner?" Then He added, "Whosoever shall fall upon that stone shall be broken; but on whomsoever it shall fall, it will grind him to powder." Luke 20:17, 18.

Christ, the Stone

More than a hundred years before Daniel's day the prophet Isaiah wrote, "Therefore thus saith the Lord God, Behold, I lay in Zion for a foundation a stone, a tried stone, a precious corner stone, a sure foundation: he that believeth shall not make haste." As Moffatt translates it, "will never flinch." Isaiah 28:16. The apostle Paul includes that Scripture in his discourse to the Romans, speaking of Christ as "a stumblingstone and rock of offence." But he adds, "Whosoever believeth in him shall not be ashamed." Romans 9:33. Peter also quotes Isaiah, applying the same text to Christ, doubtless remembering the occasion when Jesus asked the disciples for their definition of Him. Peter had replied, "Thou art the Christ, the Son of the living God." To which our Lord replied, "Upon this rock I will build my church." That is, upon the deity of the Son of God so clearly confessed by Simon Peter. Upon that solid rock of truth the church is established. Matthew 16:16-18.

Writing to the Corinthian believers, Paul reminds them that Israel "did all eat the same spiritual meat; and did all drink the same spiritual drink: for they drank of that spiritual Rock that followed them: and that Rock was Christ." 1 Corinthians 10:3, 4. Yes, our Lord is the rock, or the stone cut out "without hands." Human generation neither fashioned His substance nor caused His appearing in the flesh. He had a human mother but no human father. He was sired not by a human male but by the Spirit of God and conceived by the virgin Mary. Seven hundred years before His birth Isaiah wrote, "Therefore the Lord himself shall give you a sign; Behold, a virgin shall conceive, and bear a son, and shall call his name Immanuel." Isaiah 7:14.

Christ Born of a Virgin

Matthew, the inspired narrator of the "kingdom messages" of Jesus, applies this prophecy to Christ. And why not? Thousands of years before our Lord's birth, the promise of God to Adam and Eve was that the woman's seed would bruise the head of Satan; victory would come through Him. Genesis 3:15. How the old rabbis pored over this statement of Scripture. What could it mean? The seed of a woman. God, to our first parents said clearly, "The seed of the woman will crush Satan's head." Not until Jesus was born of a virgin could we fully understand that promise.

Paul emphasizes that supreme miracle when he says, "but when the fulness of the time was come, God sent forth his Son, made of a woman." Note how precise the Scripture is; not made of a man and a woman like the rest of us, but "made of a woman." The human male had nothing to do with our Lord's birth. It was a physiological miracle to meet a physiological, psychological, and desperate spiritual need—the redemption of a lost race.

That One born of Mary whose father is the Almighty God is "the stone of Israel," the spiritual rock, "the stone . . . cut out without hands." That stone will strike the image on the feet, dashing it to pieces, and then fill the whole earth.

Let us return to Daniel's interpretation: "Whereas thou sawest the feet and toes, part of potters' clay, and part of iron, the kingdom shall be divided; but there shall be in it of the strength of the iron, forasmuch as thou sawest the iron mixed with miry clay. And as the toes of the feet were part of iron, and part of clay, so the kingdom shall be partly strong, and partly broken (*brittle*, RSV)."

We have already noted the significance of that expression, "they shall mingle themselves with the seed of men: but they shall not cleave one to another, even as iron is not mixed with clay." Those words in Daniel 2:41-43 have stood the test of centuries. Time was when Queen Victoria of England was the grandmother and King Christian of Denmark was the grandfather of most of the crowned heads of Europe. But after World War I nearly all the monarchies of Europe had vanished. Europe is still divided, some nations strong, others weak. Nothing on earth can weld them into a permanent unity. They will remain divided until the appearing of our Lord Jesus, who comes to reign forever as King of kings and Lord of lords.

When May We Expect Christ's Return?

Is there any way of knowing when we might expect our Lord to come? Yes, there is. The same great prophecy of Daniel says that "in the days of these kings [the divided nations of Europe] shall the God of heaven set up a kingdom, which shall never be destroyed." Verse 44.

When the prophet speaks of "these kings," he makes himself quite clear. Some commentators suggest it might be the kings of the four universal empires—Babylon, Medo-Persia, Greece, and Rome. But the stone does not strike the Babylonian head nor the Medo-Persian breast and arms. It does not strike the Grecian thighs of brass or the iron legs of Rome. It is to strike the *feet and toes* at the very time the nations are trying desperately to unite divided Europe. It could well be that in this generation, while men try frantically to solve the European problem by the Common Market, that the stone will strike and the kingdom of God will come. Many other prophecies reveal that these are indeed the latter days.

This prophetic message thunders its message in our ears: *There will be no more world empires.* Several times during the last two centuries it seemed likely that the kingdoms would be welded, but every such effort has failed.

"It looked as if Napoleon would conquer the civilized world and the prophecy prove to be untrue. But the waters of the Berezina engulfed his battalions and the silent, soft, falling snow was a winding sheet around half of his army that perished on the steppes of Russia. The other half of his noble and gallant men lay with their bones bleaching or their bodies buried on the plains of Waterloo. The august invincible emporer . . . [became] a refugee and an exile to die alone on the rocky island of Helena. Why? Because God had said 600 years before Christ and 2500 years before Napoleon was born, that after the Roman empire there would never be another universal dominion."—W. A. Criswell, *Expository Sermons on the Book of Daniel,* Vol. 2, p. 77.

Napoleon was not the stone that would shatter the kingdoms. But there is a stone, a mystic, destroying stone that will strike, leaving nothing.

When the Stone Strikes

Bible prophecy not only makes clear *when* the stone shall strike but also *how* and *what* will happen. "It shall break in pieces and consume all these kingdoms," said the prophet, "and it shall stand for ever." Verse 44. It will not be a gradual, imperceptible breaking. The psalmist says, "Our God shall come, and shall not keep silence: a fire shall devour before him, and it shall be very tempestuous round about him. He shall call to the heavens from above, and to the earth, that he may judge his people." Psalm 50:3, 4. The prophet John, catching a vision of that glorious event, writes: "And the heavens departed as a scroll when it is rolled together; and every mountain and island were moved out of their places. And the kings of the earth, and the great men, and the rich men, and the chief captains, and the mighty men, and every bondman, and every free man, hid themselves in the dens and in the rocks of the mountains; and said to the mountains and rocks, Fall on us, and hide us from the face of him that sitteth on the throne, and from the wrath of the Lamb: for the great day of his wrath is come; and who shall be able to stand?" Revelation 6:14-17.

Some, however, will be able to stand, for we read: "God is our refuge and strength, a very present help in trouble. Therefore will not we fear, though the earth be removed, and though the mountains be carried into the midst of the sea." "The heathen raged, the kingdoms were moved: he uttered his voice, the earth melted." "Come, behold the works of the Lord, what desolations he hath made in the earth. He maketh wars to cease unto the end of the earth; he breaketh the bow, and cutteth the spear in sunder; he burneth the chariot in the fire." "The Lord of hosts is with us; the God of Jacob is our refuge." Psalm 46:1, 2, 6, 8, 9, 11. How relevant are the words of our Lord, who said to the scribes and Pharisees, "Whosoever shall fall on this stone shall be broken: but on whomsoever it shall fall, it will grind him to powder." Matthew 21:44.

The apostle Paul says, "The Lord Jesus shall be revealed from heaven with his mighty angels, . . . taking vengeance on them that know not God, and that obey not the gospel of our Lord Jesus Christ: who shall be punished with everlasting destruction from the presence of the Lord, and from the glory of his power; when he shall come to be glorified in his saints." 2 Thessalonians 1:7-10.

In his dream Nebuchadnezzar saw what was left of all the earthly powers blown away and no place found for them. "And the stone that smote the image became [grew into] a great mountain and filled the whole earth."

No more striking symbol could have been selected to impress the Chaldean monarch. Centuries before Nebuchadnezzar and his illustrious father Nabopolassar came to power and rebuilt the ancient city of Babylon, making it the capital of the Neo-Babylonian Empire, Nippur was one of the chief cities of Babylonia; there was the shrine of the Sumerian god Enlil, "god of the lands," sometimes called the "the stone god." The Amorite kings, of whom Ham-

murabi was chief, replaced the god Enlil with Marduk, or Merodach, who then became the supreme god of Babylon. Enlil was no
longer the god of lordship and the lands. In fact, he is pictured as
bestowing on Marduk his favor and place of honor and "his own
title, 'Lord of the lands.' . . . From this time forward Merodach
was looked upon as the 'Enlil of the gods.'"—Charles Boutflower,
In and Around the Book of Daniel, page 95.

Digging in the ruins of Babylon, archaeologists found the name
Shadu Rabu on many cuneiform inscriptions. This name was originally associated with Enlil, and his main temple in the ancient city
of Nippur meant "a great mountain." This was known as "the house
of the great mountain of the land." Nippur was recognized as the
religious center of Babylonia. When Nebuchadnezzar's armies centuries later overran Nippur, they interpreted that as evidence that
Marduk, or Merodach, was stronger than Enlil. So Nebuchadnezzar
applied the name *Shadu Rabu* to Marduk, the supreme god of
Babylon.

Another meaning of Enlil was "lord of the storm" or "storm of
terrible strength." In Babylonian mythology, Tiamat the dragon
of chaos was overcome by Marduk, who launched an attack against
her, sending against this god a "sevenfold wind or a whirlwind." So
when Daniel spoke to Nebuchadnezzar about a great wind and a
great mountain, this was familiar language to the king. The young
Hebrew's interpretation had a peculiar significance not only to the
king but also to any others who heard the explanation. The language was most appropriate. No figures could possible have been
used that could have had a greater influence. According to Jastrow,
"the sacred edifices of Babylonia were intended to be imitations of
mountains." Even "the earth itself" was pictured as a "great mountain."—*Religion of Babylonia and Assyria,* M. Jastrow, 1898 ed.,
p. 614.

Mystic Stone Kingdom Soon to Be Established

The political sovereignty of the world, at that time in Babylon,
the head of gold, was to pass to others and then to still others until
at last the sovereignty of the God of heaven would replace the
powers of the whole world. The stone kingdom will be an everlasting kingdom which shall never be destroyed, said Daniel. It will

fill the whole earth and stand unchallenged forever and ever.

King Nebuchadnezzar bowed before Daniel in reverent worship, recognizing that Daniel's God was indeed the God of the universe. He said, "Of a truth it is, that your God is a God of gods, and a Lord of kings, and a revealer of secrets." Daniel 2:47. Daniel was made "regent over the whole province of Babylon and chief prefect over all the wise men of Babylon." Verse 48, NEB.

Think of this brilliant young Chaldean king, master of a great empire, bowing reverently in worship because of what had been revealed to him. Is the same kind of reverent response in our hearts as we review this prophecy? We are twenty-five centuries removed from the scene, and the stone kingdom which will replace the kingdoms of this world is about to be established. If that kingdom of glory were to be ushered in now, would we be ready? Could we take our place as citizens of heaven, members of the family of God? If not, then let us settle that question right now, before we read any farther.

In these tremendous days when thousands are turning from darkness to light and accepting our Lord as Saviour and coming King, let us decide that at all costs we will be among those to whom the Lord will say, "Come, ye blessed of my Father, inherit the kingdom prepared for you from the foundation of the world." Matthew 25:34.

6
Treason, Trial, and Triumph

The story of the Babylonian protesters who were thrown into the furnace is well known. While many today regard the story as legend, yet the writer of the New Testament epistle to the Hebrews includes it in his list of evidences of faith. Referring to Daniel and his three companions, the writer mentions those "who through faith . . . quenched the violence of fire" and also "stopped the mouth of lions." Through "righteousness" these men "obtained promises." Hebrews 11:33, 34. An inspired New Testament record therefore seals these accounts as true.

These are more than children's stories. They are revelations of God's power to deliver His servants who put their trust in Him. The central figure in the story of the fiery furnace is neither the king nor the courageous Hebrews, but the Son of God whom the king saw walking in the fire. What marvelous overtones there are in this narrative. Paul probably had such experiences in mind when he wrote, "For whatsoever things were written aforetime were written for our learning, that we through patience and comfort of the scriptures might have hope." Romans 15:4.

When the king of Babylon set up his golden image on the plain of Dura, his reputation as conqueror and ruler had been established. No date is known for the episode of the great image, but it certainly occurred after Nebuchadnezzar was firmly established on his throne. Earlier the king had heard the interpretation of the dream of the metallic image, showing that the head of gold represented Nebuchadnezzar and his kingdom.

During the years since the dream Nebuchadnezzar had conquered other kingdoms. He was a real success. There is no record that he ever lost a battle. Pride and ambition now urged him to erect a monument to his own greatness which would impress the world that Babylon would be indestructible—a kingdom which would break in pieces other kingdoms and stand forever.

A few years ago archaeologists discovered a mound on which are found the remains of a rectangular brick structure. Some believe this might well have been the base of this huge golden image. The measurements recorded in Daniel are given in the sexagesimal system. It was sixty cubits (about 90 feet) high including the base, and six cubits (9 feet) broad. The Babylonians used this system founded on the number sixty. It is divisible by twelve factors, in contrast with our system founded on the number one hundred, which is divisible by only nine factors. We still follow the sexagesimal system in the measurement of time (and angles)—sixty seconds make a minute, sixty minutes an hour (or a degree).

Gathering of Administrators

Administrative leaders attending this great ceremony came from many parts of the growing empire. The occasion was a dedication ceremony. Although not primarily a religious gathering, religion played an important role in almost everything the Babylonians did. No priests or philosophers or astrologers are mentioned as being present, but the governors, captains, judges, treasurers, counselors, and rulers of provinces were required to attend. This pageant was designed to impress everybody with the glory of Babylon.

At the time of the dream of Daniel 2, Shadrach, Meshach, and Abednego, the three Hebrews mentioned in the story, had been appointed as administrative leaders. Daniel 2:49. Thus they were present at the ceremony. And there was no mistaking the royal order: "When you hear the sound of the horn, pipe, lyre, trigon, harp, bagpipe, and every kind of music, you are to fall down and worship the golden image that King Nebuchadnezzar has set up. And whoever does not fall down and worship shall immediately be cast into a burning fiery furnace." Daniel 3:4-6, RSV.

Refusal to obey the king's order was treason. The situation was important and the atmosphere tense. To understand the real issues involved, we must see this as one of the unusual ways God chose to reveal truth to Babylon.

That day on the plain of Dura two invisible powers met head on—the power of earthly ambition inspired by the prince of darkness and the power of love revealed in the lives of men dedicated to truth and righteousness. The charge brought against these men as recorded in verse 12 is revealing. It is easy to see a spirit of jealousy moving some to say to the king, "Certain Jews whom thou hast set over the affairs of the province . . . have not regarded thee." A herald had summoned all "people, nations and languages" to heed the mandate and bow in homage before the golden image, a symbol of man's greatness. This the loyal Hebrews could not conscientiously do. They held in respect the king, as is shown in their reply. But they had to protest.

Nebuchadnezzar was embarrassed and enraged. He ordered the three men to appear before him. He had never had cause to doubt their loyalty before. He knew, of course, that they did not worship his gods. From his point of view he was not really asking them to abandon the worship of their God. All he required was that they bow in recognition of his symbol of the fact that Babylon was the greatest and most enduring power on earth. But these men recognized a greater power—that of Jehovah.

To disobey the king's order was treason punishable by death. But Nebuchadnezzar, eager to spare their lives, offered to give them another chance. They did not need another chance. The issue was perfectly plain to them. So they courteously replied: "We would not make any defense in this matter; for our God whom we serve is able to save us." Verse 16, Berkeley. They knew that either God would deliver them from death or in death.

What a marvelous example of faith in the living God! They rested their case with Him. More than a hundred years earlier the prophet Isaiah had penned the promise, "When thou passest through the waters, I will be with thee; . . . when thou walkest through the fire, thou shalt not be burned; neither shall the flame kindle upon thee." Isaiah 43:2. Wrapped in such a promise, they could give their witness confidently.

If we put ourselves in the place of Nebuchadnezzar, we can appreciate his problem. To have permitted these men to defy him would have seriously affected his standing as ruler. His position before the world was at stake. He commanded the furnace to be heated "seven times" hotter than usual, and that these men dressed in all their gay regalia—their trousers, shirts, mantles, and turbans —be bound and hurled into the flames. Moreover, the strongest men of the army were chosen for the grim execution. Picked up like living logs, these protesters were tossed into the blazing furnace. The flame "slew those men who took up Shadrach, Meshach, and Abed-nego." Daniel 3:22.

"That has put an end to the matter," Nebuchadnezzar no doubt thought. But when man has done his worst, God can always add a final chapter. And what a chapter it was! In his fury Nebuchadnezzar had challenged Jehovah: "Who is that God that shall deliver you out of *my* hands?" Verse 15. But he did not realize the power he was opposing. In a matter of minutes this autocratic king got the revelation of his life. He saw the God that he had defied walking in the fire with His three faithful servants. That was a theophany, a preincarnate appearance of our Lord who later was born in Bethlehem.

Not only did the king see this miracle, but so also did his administrative leaders—governors, rulers, treasurers, counselors. The fire which slew the executioners had no power over the men they had thought to destroy. Not a hair of their head was singed, nor was the smell of fire upon them. Verse 27. Only the cords that bound them were burned.

Moving nearer the furnace, Nebuchadnezzar called to them: "Ye servants of the most high God, come forth, and come hither." Verse 26. "The most high God" was a reverent name evidently well known to the king. The term "most high" is found eight times in the first five chapters of Daniel. Nebuchadnezzar had heard also about angels, for later he confessed that God had "sent his angel, and delivered his servants that trusted in him." Verse 28. These men had yielded their bodies but not their wills. We get a glimpse of Nebuchadnezzar as a man with a certain greatness of soul, for he even rejoiced that his own word had been changed. "There is no other God that can deliver after this sort." Verse 29.

So overwhelmed was Nebuchadnezzar by this revelation of divine power that he decided to go into partnership with this God. He even made a decree granting recognition to the Hebrew religion, and he pledged protection for the God of Shadrach, Meshach, and

Abednego. Any who opposed Him should be "cut in pieces," as if Jehovah needed human protection! The king published a royal document telling of this marvelous deliverance, and he sent this throughout the empire. Thus the name and power of Jehovah were proclaimed. This was God's second message to Babylon.

The story ends in a doxology of praise, in an atmosphere of toleration which prepared the way for God's third message to Babylon. This we will note in our next chapter. These brave men, instead of being destroyed, were "promoted." Their humble courage in the face of bitter opposition has inspired countless thousands throughout the centuries. We do well to study the example of these noble men in these days when loyalty is often regarded as obstinacy.

John Chrysostom was one of the great Greek church fathers. Born in A.D. 347, he was brought before the Emperor at an early age to answer for his faith.

"If you persist in being a Christian" said the emperor, "I will banish you from your father's land."

Chrysostom replied, "Your Majesty, you cannot; the whole world is my Father's land."

"Then I will take away all your property,"

"You cannot do that either. My treasures are in heaven."

"Then I will send you to a place where there will not be a friend to speak to."

"You cannot do that, for I have a Friend that sticketh closer than a brother. I shall have my Brother Jesus Christ forever."

The emperor said, "I will take away your life."

"You cannot do that either. My life is hid with Christ in God," Chrysostom answered.

That was not blind obstinacy. It was faith—"the faith of Jesus" which will characterize the last witnesses of God's true church on earth. Revelation 14:12. We need such faith today.

As boys, Shadrach, Meshach, and Abednego had been brought up on the Ten Commandments, the first of which says, "Thou shalt have no other gods before me." The second is an expansion of the first. "Thou shalt not make unto thee any graven image . . . : thou shalt not bow down thyself to them, nor serve them: for I the Lord thy God am a jealous God." Now they were men—governors of provinces in the empire of Babylon.

When they had arrived in Babylon, the king changed their names, but he could not change their devotion to the living God. They were members of a conquered race; and, when they appeared before Nebuchadnezzar, they realized that they were standing before the conqueror. Yet they were unconquerable. Having seen by faith the face of God, they need not fear the face of man. As we read the story in Daniel, chapter three, we note that their names are repeated thirteen times in this one chapter. There was no mistaking the three to whom the king was speaking. Everyone present knew who these men were. All eyes turned to witness men who would dare to disobey the king. But before the day ended, the whole retinue of Babylonian leaders knew that with these Hebrews there was no compromise.

It is easy in such a situation to rationalize. Some might have reasoned that a simple genuflection was little enough to do for a king who had treated them so kindly. Others might say in the words of Solomon, "a living dog is better than a dead lion," or in today's lingo, "better to be Red than dead." But these men could not compromise, for they were first God's servants and second servants of Nebuchadnezzar. We can almost hear them reciting the words of Joshua, "As for me and my house, we will serve the Lord" (Joshua 24:15), or the words of David, "My heart is fixed, O God, my heart is fixed." Psalm 57:7.

They knew He could deliver; however, they went on to add, "but if not—" How hard those words are to say! God does not always intervene in such a miraculous way. And we can well imagine the emotions of these men as the fire was heated seven times hotter, and the assembled host expected the end of these stubborn Jews. What a surprise awaited that crowd!

In setting up this image, all of gold, Nebuchadnezzar was challenging God's plan of history as revealed in the dream of four successive empires and the final establishment of God's everlasting kingdom. Babylon's king was determined that his kingdom would continue; the golden kingdom was to endure forever.

But God's deliverance of His servants "changed the king's word," as He can change any and all who challenge His right to rule.

7
Maniac King Regains His Kingdom

We have already noticed that the book of Daniel is an apocalyptic book, divided equally between history and prophecy. It is not a complete history of Babylon or the captive Jews, for it touches only those events which definitely affected the people of God. The whole Bible follows this pattern. The first eleven chapters of Genesis cover the creation of the world, the fall of man, the destruction of the world by flood. Then the record touches the development of philosophies such as that which led to the building of the tower of Babel, which led men far away from God. Chapters 12 to 28 trace the history of Abraham and Isaac. The last twenty-two chapters give the history of Jacob and his family especially of Joseph.

Secular history is not usually this way. While there is much history in the Bible, the whole purpose of the Sacred Book is to reveal the gospel of salvation to men. God's purpose through Abraham's posterity was "to carry true religion to the nations." Isaiah 42:1, Moffatt. To accomplish this, the Lord used not only the faithful witness of His people but even the scattering of Israel and Judah.

Gentile nations overran Palestine during the sixth and seventh centuries B.C., Assyria taking Israel into captivity and Babylon overthrowing Judah. We might wonder if anything good could come out of such conquests. But wherever Israel and Judah were scattered they carried with them some knowledge of the true God.

Nebuchadnezzar in Varied Roles

In the first three chapters of Daniel, King Nebuchadnezzar is portrayed as a *conqueror,* an *autocrat,* and a *builder.* But in the fourth we find him a *converted servant* of the most high God. More is recorded in sacred history about this man than perhaps any other Gentile ruler. In Daniel, chapter 3, we saw Nebuchadnezzar as an autocrat defying the God of heaven. But the monarch's word was changed. Years later in the document preserved in Daniel, chapter 4, he says, "I . . . was at rest . . . , and flourishing in my palace." Verse 4. And that was no mere figure of speech. This proud conqueror and prouder architect had accomplished much. The royal document recorded in chapter 4 he sent throughout the lands under his authority. In this he related his own experience.

His conquests were at an end. The empire was consolidated. The city of Babylon was adorned with lofty palaces. He had created one of the seven wonders of the world—the hanging gardens, built in his wife's honor. The city contained 53 dedicated temples, 955 smaller sanctuaries, and 384 altars. Werner Keller describes "Babylon as an international center of trade, industry and commerce."—*The Bible as History*, page 297.

Nebuchadnezzar, the Builder

Nebuchadnezzar's last compaign against Egypt ended his military career. God gave him Egypt as "wages for his army" because of the service he had rendered against Tyre. His siege against Tyre lasted thirteen years. The Scripture says, "Nebuchadrezzar king of Babylon caused his army to serve a great service against Tyrus: every head was made bald, and every shoulder was peeled: yet had he no wages, nor his army, for Tyrus, for the service that he had served against it: therefore thus saith the Lord God; Behold, I will give the land of Egypt unto Nebuchadrezzar king of Babylon; . . . and it shall be the wages for his army. I have given him the land of Egypt for his labour wherewith he served against it, because they wrought for me, saith the Lord God." Ezekiel 29:18-20.

Apparently Nebuchadnezzar invaded Egypt and carried away rich booty. From all the conquered countries, including Judah and the other nations of that area, he brought gold and art treasures to adorn the city of Babylon, hailed as "the golden city" and "the glory of kingdoms." Isaiah 14:4; 13:19. There was much to admire in Nebuchadnezzar. To those who accepted his rule, he was beneficent. The Jewish captives he treated kindly, leading Jeremiah, the prophet of God, to counsel the refugees to "build . . . houses" and "plant gardens" and to "seek the peace of the city." Jeremiah 29:5-7. The area around Babylon was devoid of stone. Consequently, for his building program Nebuchadnezzar needed brick. He therefore made Babylon the center of the greatest brick-making industry of his times. This ruler became one of the greatest builders of antiquity. Boutflower says, "He seems to have been possessed with a perfect rage for building." "My heart impelled me" are his own expressive words.—*In and Around the Book of Daniel,* page 68.

Nebuchadnezzar as Woodsman

One of Nebuchadnezzar's royal inscriptions reads, "I made the inhabitants of the Lebanon live in safety together and let nobody disturb them."—James B. Pritchard, *Ancient New Eastern Texts,* page 307.

The monarch of Babylon was particularly fond of great cedars, which he brought all the way from the mountains of Lebanon. He regarded the forests of Lebanon as the possession of his Babylonian god Marduk. He tells us he "cut through steep mountains" to open up the way for "mighty cedars, high and strong," to be transported into Babylon.—*Ibid.*

In the document preserved in Daniel, chapter 4, he says: "I . . . was at rest." No longer was he leading his armies to victory or was he building beautiful palaces. His developing days were over. Probably no single man ever left behind him as his memorial upon the earth one half the amount of building that was erected by this king.

Now for the story: The king again had an impressive dream. As before, the dream left him deeply troubled. Calling the magicians, the astrologers, the Chaldeans, and the soothsayers, he related the dream to them. But again he was disappointed. They could give no interpretation. Then "at the last Daniel came." Nebuchadnezzar's attitude toward Daniel is quite touching. He called him "master of the magicians," saying, "The spirit of the holy gods is in thee, and no secret troubleth thee." Verse 9.

The important events of this dream "made me afraid," he said. Nebuchadnezzar afraid? He had conquered nations and yet this dream left him staggered. In the dream (verses 10-17) he saw an immense tree which seemed to reach to "the end of all the earth." And under its branches the beasts of the field and the fowls of the heaven found shelter. Then he heard a voice saying, "Hew down the tree, and cut off his branches, shake off his leaves, and scatter his fruit: . . . nevertheless leave the stump of his roots in the earth, even with a band of iron and brass . . . : let his heart be changed from man's, and let a beast's heart be given unto him; and let seven times pass over him." This declaration was to inform everyone "the most High ruleth in the kingdom of men, and giveth it to whomsoever he will, and setteth up over it the basest of men."

When Daniel heard it, he too was troubled. A whole hour passed in silence. While the king was concerned, Daniel was even more concerned; for during the two or three decades of very close association these two men, the king and the prime minister, had become close associates. At last the king said, "Let not the dream, or the interpretation thereof, trouble thee." But Daniel knew the interpretation would come as a shock, and thus the silence.

Daniel Interprets the Dream

The prophet begins: "My lord, the dream be to them that hate thee, and the interpretation thereof to thine enemies." He has a solemn message with a very personal application, and he must give it to one for whom he has great regard. "It is thou, O king, that art grown and become strong: for thy greatness is grown . . . to the end of the earth." Respectfully, he says: "Whereas the king saw a watcher and an holy one coming down from heaven, and saying, Hew the tree down, and destroy it; . . . and let his portion be with the beasts of the field, till seven times pass over him; this is the interpretation, O king, and this is the decree of the most High."

Continuing, the statesman-prophet unfolded God's message: "They shall drive thee from men, and thy dwelling shall be with the beasts of the field, and they shall make thee to eat grass as oxen, . . . and seven times [seven years] shall pass over thee, till thou know that the most High ruleth in the kingdom of men, and giveth it to whomsoever he will."

It was not easy to bear a clear prophetic message to this proud, autocratic ruler. Daniel loved Nebuchadnezzar and doubtless had been praying for many years that in some way this great general, this great builder, this outstanding leader of men would come to know that "the heavens do rule." What a different world this would be if the rulers of all nations recognized that, in spite of their greatness, their power and prestige, a greater power is still in charge! The everlasting God rules earth and heaven.

Daniel as Friend, Prophet, and Evangelist

Now Daniel the prophet becomes Daniel the evangelist. Listen as he pleads for this man's soul: "Wherefore, O king, let my counsel be acceptable unto thee, and break off thy sins by righteousness, and thine iniquities by shewing mercy to the poor; if it may be a lengthening of thy tranquillity"—or as Moffatt says, "perhaps your prosperity may be prolonged."

Many today, after hearing bad news, are sobered for a while. But as the months pass, the Holy Spirit's impressions are brushed aside. So it was with Nebuchadnezzar—his heart was not transformed. He still indulged a spirit of self-glorification, and perhaps even jested about his former fears. To himself he said: "Babylon was built by me alone, by my might, for my majesty."

The King's Mind Snaps

Exactly one year after Daniel's appeal, while boasting of his greatness, the king's mind suddenly snapped; he was a maniac. Unexpectedly, God struck down his proud impiety. His greatness and glory meant nothing now. Said the voice: "The kingdom is departed from thee."

Despite his position and his regal glory, he fled from the palace to the field, smitten with madness, suffering from a disease known to medical science as "lycanthropy" (*lukos,* wolf and *anthropos,* man) "a delusion that one has become or has assumed the characteristics of a wolf or other predatory animal." Is such a strange illness possible? The *Dictionary of Psychological Medicine* declares "the complete loss of personal identity and the conviction of being changed into one of the lower animals . . . is one of the most remarkable facts in psychological history that the race reveals."—Quoted in *Studies of the Book of Daniel,* by Dr. Robert Dick Wilson, pages 286, 287.

Nebuchadnezzar Returns to the Throne

Daniel was probably there when the king lost his reason, and thus was able to counsel those responsible for affairs of state. He knew just how long it would be until the king's mind would be restored. But let Nebuchadnezzar tell the story. One of the most remarkable passages in all the Bible is Daniel 4:34-37, where the king says: "At the end of the days I Nebuchadnezzar lifted up mine eyes unto heaven, and mine understanding returned unto me, and I blessed the most High, and I praised and honoured him." Daniel 4:34. What a change! No longer did he consider himself a beast; he was a man!

How did Nebuchadnezzar know he had reached "the end of the days"? During those years he had had no knowledge of time or human responsibilities. In his royal document he says, "my counsellors and my lords sought unto me." Naturally his counsellors would surround him after he was reinstated, but let us imagine the part Daniel must have played in the affairs of the government during those long years of waiting.

The King Comes Home

Knowing the purpose of God, the prophet-statesman doubtless looked forward to the time when the king would return in his right mind. The queen also may have helped preserve the nation. She was a princess from the mountain region of Media, and on this lady the king had lavished much. He built the "hanging gardens" for her pleasure. But now "at the end of the days," what can the queen and the counsellors expect? Will the king return? If so, how? It does not take much imagination to see Daniel at the head of a chosen group going to the field or the forest in search of his friend.

Knowing the king's haunts, Daniel makes his way till he finally locates him. With a prayer of praise to God that the seven years are at an end, he walks up to this creature who, though human, has thought of himself as an animal. Daniel lifts his eyes heavenward as he addresses God, the same God who has answered his prayers during the twenty or thirty years since he first faced King Nebuchadnezzar. But what a contrast now! This beastlike human is covered with filth, his matted hair dangling on the ground and his nails grown like birds' claws—a repulsive sight. But now Nebuchadnezzar lifts his eyes to heaven and opens his heart to the God of gods whose "dominion is an everlasting dominion . . . and all the inhabitants of the earth are reputed as nothing." He begins to realize that the living God "doeth according to his will in the army of heaven [the angels], and among the inhabitants of the earth: and none can stay his hand, or say unto him, What doest thou?" Verses 34, 35.

Having been exposed to the elements for years, Nebuchadnezzar is a strange sight. But his heart is radiant and joyful. "Now I Nebuchadnezzar praise and extol and honour the King of heaven, all whose works are truth, and his ways judgment: and those that walk in pride he is able to abase." Verse 37.

How wonderful that a heathen autocrat could learn the saving truth of righteousness by faith! Daniel, who had prayed for this man's salvation for many years, now has the joy of witnessing his conversion.

Babylon's Spirit in Today's World

In the dream Nebuchadnezzar had seen the stump of the tree bound by two bands, one of iron, the other of brass. In the metallic image of chapter 2, we reflect that the brass represented Greece; and the iron, Rome. The tree Nebuchadnezzar saw in his dream represented not only the king as a person but Babylon as a system. Daniel's interpretation emphasized that the influence of Babylon's kingdom reached "to the end of the earth." The spirit of Babylon which began under Nimrod's rulership some sixteen centuries earlier with the building of the tower of Babel, and also a number of important cities (see Genesis 10:12; 11:1-9), had spread out and gripped the whole world. And that spirit did not die with Nebuchadnezzar. Even today's world is under the strong influence of the mystery religions of ancient Babylon.

Nebuchadnezzar's royal document was sent to "all people, nations, and languages." Daniel 4:1. This may be thought of as hyperbole, but the influence of Babylon was doubtless felt in many of the unconquered lands. The king said, "For the glory of my kingdom, mine honour and brightness returned unto me; . . . I was established in my kingdom, and excellent majesty was added unto me."

Concluding, he gives his own personal testimony, a doxology, "Now I Nebuchadnezzar praise and extol and honour the King of heaven, all whose works are truth, and his ways judgment: and those that walk in pride he is able to abase." Verse 37. Not only does he recognize the justice of his affliction, but he praises the God of truth for His mercy and justice. This sobered, converted king ruled for perhaps two years before he passed to his rest.

The genuineness of his conversion is seen by his willingness to tell the story, including the details of his own folly and the marvelous grace of the everlasting God. How wonderful that God by His grace could take a seemingly hopeless case like this proud king and make him a member of the family of God! When God undertakes to abase our pride and lay human glory in the dust, that is truly a work of creation just as when He brought this earth from chaos to beauty. All this is portrayed in this unusual royal document. Will it not be a privilege in the coming kingdom of glory to fellowship with Nebuchadnezzar and hear from the man himself the story of God's patience and love?

Worldly Wisdom Rejects the Gospel

Twenty-seven years after Nebuchadnezzar died, the empire of Babylon passed away forever. The Babylonian principles, however, were not uprooted when the empire fell, but were preserved by the Greeks and the Romans. Greece became the home of great philosophers, educators, artists, and sculptors, but God as Creator and Sustainer was not recognized in it all. The Greeks sought to develop a superrace. Sculpture reached its highest point in Athens, with special reverence for the human form. "A mutilated body is an impertinency," they said. No wonder it was so difficult to reach the Greek mind with the gospel of a crucified Christ. How, they reasoned, could One who permitted Himself to be taken by His enemies be man's Saviour? So the people of Paul's day turned away from the saving grace of Christ. The apostle Paul observed that "the world by wisdom knew not God." 1 Corinthians 1:21.

Rome's contribution to culture was more in the field of law and government. What philosophy they had came largely from Greece. Like Babylon's rule, Rome's rule was also autocratic. The world became a prison from which there was no escape.

"History repeats itself," we say, and that seems to be true. Much that characterized ancient Babylon is being reenacted in our day. In Revelation 13:15, we read of the "beast" (modern Babylon) and his "image" (apostate Christianity) uniting to oppose God's people in the last days. In the name of human development and international peace demands will be made on all the world to worship the beast and his image. Those who refuse will face a death decree. But the same God who delivered His ancient servants who put their trust in Him will deliver His people in the final worldwide test.

Daniel Speaks to Our Day

Not only the prophecies of Daniel, but also the historic sections have special meaning for us in these days. Well did the apostle Paul say, "Whatsoever things were written aforetime were written for our learning, that we through patience and comfort of the scriptures might have hope." Romans 15:4. This counsel from Ellen White should challenge every lover of God's Word:

"There is need of a much closer study of the word of God; especially should Daniel and the Revelation have attention as never before in the history of our work. We may have less to say in some lines, in regard to the Roman power and the papacy; but we should call attention to what the prophets and apostles have written under the inspiration of the Holy Spirit of God. The Holy Spirit has so shaped matters, both in the giving of the prophecy and in the events portrayed, as to teach that the human agent is to be kept out of sight, hid in Christ, and that the Lord God of heaven and His law are to be exalted. Read the book of Daniel. Call up, point by point, the history of the kingdoms there represented. Behold statesmen, councils, powerful armies, and see how God wrought to abase the pride of men, and lay human glory in the dust.

"The light that Daniel received from God was given especially for these last days. The visions he saw by the banks of the Ulai and the Hiddekel, the great rivers of Shinar, are now in process of fulfillment, and all the events foretold will soon come to pass."—*Testimonies to Ministers*, pages 112, 113.

May the Spirit of God, who inspired these records, guide us as we further study these prophecies.

8
Belshazzar
and Babylon's Fall

Was there ever such a man as Belshazzar, or is he just a legendary figure? For many years some regarded him as a fictitious character. But today, thanks to archaeology, we know not only that he existed but that he and his father Nabonidus were vital characters in the unfolding story of nations.

The fall of Babylon, one of the greatest and most beautiful cities of ancient times, has left an indelible mark on history. The overthrow of this Chaldean Empire by the Persians fulfilled a number of prophecies well-known to Daniel. Nothing that happened on that tragic night recorded in Daniel 5 came as a surprise to him. He knew what Isaiah and Jeremiah had foretold concerning the city. Some of those prophecies we will notice in detail later, but first the story of the fall.

Nabonidus, Belshazzar's father, ascended the throne in 555 B.C.; he made Belshazzar a coruler in about 553 B.C. Nabonidus, more of a scholar than a military leader, has been called "the first archaeologist." His inscriptions indicate that he was also deeply religious. Belshazzar was reckless and defiant. At the time the city fell he was engaging in a wild party with a thousand of his lords. Babylon's fall brought an end to a dynasty that had started so promisingly.

Belshazzar's Defiant Feast

That hilarious night of drunkenness and idolatry was, according to the famous Nabonidus Chronicle in the British Museum, the eve of the great days of celebration—the sixteenth of Tishri. Belshazzar's defiance of the God of heaven reached an all-time high on that occasion. When liquor had dethroned reason, he commanded that the sacred vessels of Jehovah, which his grandfather Nebuchadnezzar had brought from Jerusalem, be brought from the sacred shrine house. From these holy vessels of God they drank the unholy wine of Babylon. The number of these gold and silver vessels, according to Ezra 1:7, 8, 11, was 5,400.

Entrenched behind tremendously high walls and surrounded by a deep moat, as described by Herodotus after his visit to the ruined city, Belshazzar felt confident that no enemy could possibly enter. He may have planned this feast to express his defiance of the advancing army of the Persians. Why should he be concerned? This city was invincible, so he thought. It had an endless supply of water from the broad River Euphrates which flowed through the center of the city. It had endless supplies of grain. It could grow ample produce inside the city, aided by irrigation. With alluvial soil and wonderful weather, the gardens could produce three crops each year.

But while Belshazzar drank and praised the gods of gold and silver and wood and bronze, he did not know that his father Nabonidus was fleeing percipitantly toward Arabia. For a kingdom to last it must be established on justice and righteousness. This orgiastic festival of impiety and immorality brought divine judgment with a suddenness that threw the whole party into consternation. Never till the moment when men or nations have filled the cup of their iniquity does God strike. Israel's possession of the land of Canaan had been delayed because "the iniquity of the Amorites was not yet full." Genesis 15:15, 16. But Babylon's cup was full to overflowing.

Letters of Fire on the Palace Wall

God bore long with the wickedness of this land, but the fateful moment came when Belshazzar stood before his lords and raised one of God's sacred cups, drinking to the gods of Babylon. While all eyes were upon the king, the assembled crowd witnessed the most startling spectacle. Out of the sleeve of darkness appeared fingers like those of a man's hand which wrote in fiery letters on the wall, "MENE, MENE, TEKEL, UPHARSIN."

The revelers hushed into silence. Was this a message of doom from another world? Was it a token of ill omen? The king called loudly for the magicians, the astrologers, the soothsayers, and the Chaldeans to explain. But they could neither read the writing nor interpret its message.

In the midst of the consternation, in came the queen mother, possibly Nitocris, daughter of Nebuchadnezzar. She reminded her blasphemous son that while the wise men could not read the writing, one in the realm could not only read the writing but also interpret it. "Let Daniel be called," she said. She remembered the part this messenger of God had played during the long reign of Nebuchadnezzar and how he led him at last to accept the Most High God. She also knew that more than sixty years earlier Daniel had stood before Nebuchadnezzar and unfolded the future of the world, declaring that Babylon would pass away and another kingdom take its place.

Daniel Interprets the Message

When Daniel appeared, the terrified monarch promised him gifts and honor. Politely, the aged statesman-prophet told the king to give his rewards to another. But "I will read the writing," he said. Before doing so, he reminded Belshazzar that it was the most high God that had given his grandfather Nebuchadnezzar a kingdom which extended to "all people, nations, and languages." "But when his heart was lifted up, and his mind hardened in pride, he was deposed from his kingly throne, and they took his glory from him: and he was driven from the sons of men; and his heart was made like the beasts, . . . till he knew that the most high God ruled in the kingdom of men, and that he appointeth over it whomsoever he will." Daniel 5:20, 21. Then, fixing his eyes on the trembling king, he delivered his message in the presence of the assembled nobles. "O Belshazzer, hast not humbled thine heart, *though thou knewest all this;* but hast lifted up thyself against the Lord of heaven." Verses 22, 23.

Belshazzar was well aware of the family history. He must have been about fourteen years old when Nebuchadnezzar died. But he had stifled his conscience. Daniel continued: "They have brought the vessels of his [the Lord's] house before thee, and thou, and thy lords, thy wives, and thy concubines, have drunk wine in them;

. . . and the God in whose hand thy breath is, and whose are all thy ways, hast thou not glorified. . . . Thou art weighed in the balances, and art found wanting. . . . Thy kingdom is divided, and given to the Medes and Persians." Verses 23-28.

Even while Daniel was reading the writing, the Persian armies were marching up the riverbed ready to enter the palace. Belshazzar's day had already passed. He had crossed the unseen barrier between God's mercy and His wrath and did not know it. He had sinned away his day of grace.

How true are the words of the wise man, "Pride goeth before destruction, and an haughty spirit before a fall." Proverbs 16:18.

The King Is Dead

The Medo-Persian troops entered the banquet hall, and soon the red blood of royalty mingled with the red wine of Babylon on the pavement of the banquet hall. Edward Arnold's well-known words fit the occasion:

> That night they slew him on his father's throne,
> The deed unnoticed and the hand unknown.
> Crownless and sceptreless, Belshazzar lay,
> A robe of purple around a form of clay.

Why could not the brilliantly educated Chaldeans read the writing? The medieval Jews believed the letters were probably placed in the form of a rectangle like this: M N A

M N A
T Q L
P R S

The words are *mene,* "to number"; *tekel,* "to weigh"; *peres,* "dividing," or *paras,* "Persian." Whatever the reason, the God of heaven planned it in order that Daniel might give his final message. That night Babylon fell to rise no more. How true are those words: "The wicked shall be turned into hell, and all the nations that forget God." Psalm 9:17.

Two of Israel's greatest prophets, Isaiah and Jeremiah, had not only predicted the downfall of Babylon; they had enumerated many of the details as to how it would be accomplished. More than a hundred years before Cyrus was born, God said through the prophet

Isaiah, "I will dry up thy rivers." Isaiah 44:27. "Thus saith the Lord to his anointed, to Cyrus . . . ; I will go before thee . . . : I will give thee the treasures of darkness, . . . I have even called thee by thy name: I have surnamed thee, though thou hast not known me." Isaiah 45:1-4.

Jeremiah, a century later than Isaiah, delivered this message from God: "A drought is upon her waters; and they shall be dried up: for it is the land of graven images, and they are mad upon their idols." Jeremiah 50:38. And again, "Babylon hath been a golden cup in the Lord's hand, that made all the earth drunken: the nations have drunken of her wine; therefore the nations are mad. Babylon is suddenly fallen and destroyed. . . . We would have healed Babylon, but she is not healed. . . . The Lord hath raised up the spirit of the kings of the Medes: for his device is against Babylon, to destroy it." Jeremiah 51:7, 9, 11. The prophet further added, "A rumour shall both come one year, and after that in an-ther year shall come a rumour, and violence in the land." Verse 46. These predictions were fulfilled in minute detail. Guided by two deserters—whom Xenophon calls Gadatus and Gobryas—the Persian conquerors made their way up the riverbed without resistance.

Cyrus Delays His Invasion

A "rumour" did come in one year that Cyrus was marching toward Babylon, but he did not arrive. The reason? It is said that while Cyrus was crossing the River Gyndes, one of his sacred white horses drawing the chariot of Ormazd (or Ahura Mazda) was drowned. Cyrus took revenge on the river, draining it into 360 channels. This took months. Not until the following year did the Persian conqueror arrive at the borders of Babylon. Then he found the conquest very different from the normal pattern. Werner Keller says, "It was without a parallel in the military practice of the ancient Orient; for this time there were no columns of smoke rising from behind shattered walls, no temples or palaces razed to the ground, no house plundered, no man was butchered or im-paled." *The Bible as History*, page 301.

In his own record Cyrus says, "As I entered Babylon in peace, and established my royal residence in the palace of the princes amid jubilation and rejoicing, Marduk [Babylon's chief god], the great lord, warmed the hearts of the Babylonians towards me." Then Cyrus tells how he freed the people from the yoke of bondage and repaired their houses, healing their afflictions. He closes by saying, "I am Cyrus, king of all, the great king, the mighty king, king of Babylon, king of Sumer and Akkad, king of the four corners of the earth."—*Ibid.*

Who Was "Darius the Median"?

Cyrus the Persian is not named in chapter five of Daniel, but "Darius the Median" is. Who was Darius the Mede? There has been considerable discussion as to his identity. In the words of Josephus, he "had another name among the Greeks."—*Antiquities* X. 11. 4. Some say he was Astyages, the last ruler of Media. Others say he was Gobryas, the governor of Babylonia under Cyrus; or even Gubaru, another governor. Still others believe he must have been Cyaxares II, son of Astyages. Whoever he was, Daniel's God recognized him and honored him, for Gabriel on one occasion was sent to Darius to "confirm and strengthen him." Daniel 11:1.

Frederick Tatford, D.D., has written that "the name Darius is not itself a proper name, but an appellative which was borne by several kings and means 'the subduer.' "—*The Climax of the Ages,* page 93. In Daniel 9:1 he is called the son of Ahasuerus. Bishop Lowth comments on this: "This is the same person who was called Cyaxares, the son of Astyages by heathen historians with whom Josephus agrees. . . . Astyages had the name of Ahasuerus among the Jews as appears by the passage in Tobit XIV, verse 15, where the taking of Nineveh is ascribed to . . . Nabopolassar, Nebuchadnezzar's father, and Astyages." Xenophon, the Greek writer, in his *Cyropaedia,* declares that Darius the Mede was Cyaxares II and therefore the son of Astyages, after whose death he became heir of the Median throne and was the last ruler, in which case his sister was Mandane, the mother of Cyrus.

Keller informs us that Astyages, Cyrus's grandfather, had two dreams which greatly troubled him. He saw water flowing from his daughter and covering great areas of the country. Fearing this to be an ill omen, he called his counselors, who assured him that the daughter's offspring was destined to overrun the whole land. Hearing that the child born to Mandane was a boy, he sent Harpagus, "the most faithful of the Medes," to destroy the baby. But this man did not have the heart for murder. The child grew and was none other than Cyrus, son of Cambyses, descendant of the royal race of Achaemenes. This royal son was greatly admired from his boyhood. "His unparalleled swift and brilliant rise to power was marred by no deed of violence," says Keller. "His able and humane policy made him one of the most attractive figures in the ancient orient. . . . Despotic cruelty was foreign to this Persian." —*The Bible as History*, page 299. He not only issued the decree permitting the Jews to return and build their temple in Jerusalem, but also bore the cost of the Jews' transportation and later of the actual construction itself.

If Cyrus was the son of Mandane, daughter of King Astyages, then her brother was Cyaxares II or Darius. This would make Darius the uncle of Cyrus, with whom the latter became well acquainted during the years he spent as a youth in the court of the Medes. After Cyrus's conquest of Babylon, he visited his uncle, presenting him with gifts. Cyaxares II, or Darius, in return gave Cyrus his daughter in marriage as well as his kingdom, according to *Cyropaedia* VIII, 5. 17, 18. It would seem, then, that Darius was not only the uncle of Cyrus, but also his father-in-law. We can therefore understand the great conqueror's inviting Darius to Babylon to act as king of that area.

Cyrus Learns of Daniel's God

Both Cyrus and Darius came to recognize Daniel's God as the God of gods. Imagine the surprise of Cyrus when, after entering the city, he learned that the God of heaven had foretold the important details of this very conquest. Daniel's influence upon the new regime must have been considerable.

The Scripture comment on the conquest is brief: "That night was Belshazzar the king of the Chaldeans slain. And Darius the Median took the kingdom, being about threescore and two years old." Daniel 5:30, 31.

Darius set up 120 princes or "satraps" over the kingdom. "And over these three presidents; of whom Daniel was first." Daniel 6:1-3. Jealousy soon arose among the two subordinate presidents and the princes, and they "sought to find occasion against Daniel concerning the kingdom." Verse 4. But the only cause they could find was concerning his religion.

After much discussion they approached Darius in a spirit of flattery and persuaded him to sign a decree according to "the law of the Medes and Persians, which altereth not." This was actually a design against Daniel, although Darius did not realize the subtlety of the plan. The wording of the decree was very clear: "Whosoever shall ask a petition of any God or man for thirty days, save of thee, O king, he shall be cast into the den of lions." Daniel 6:7.

The Persians, like other Orientals, regarded the king as divine and worshiped him as the representative of Ormazd, or Ahura Mazda. So the plan was not unusual. But it was all a trap for Daniel, and Daniel knew it. But he could not be intimidated. He still carried out his regular worship, "his windows being opened." He knelt "three times a day, and prayed." Verse 10. Had he closed the windows, that would have shown cowardice. Of course he could have rationalized, "Well, I can pray in my heart. God will understand." But Daniel was no compromiser. He knew that those men were waiting and watching, and they soon had a clear case.

Coming to Darius, they remined him of the decree he had signed. Then they made the charge saying, "That Daniel, which is of the children of the captivity of Judah, regardeth not thee, O king, nor the decree that thou hast signed, but maketh his petition three times a day." Verse 13.

It was then that Darius realized what his perfidious courtiers had done. He was alarmed and deeply grieved. He knew he had been trapped. All day long he labored, hoping to find a way out, consulting with lawyers and politicians, but without success. The statute could not be changed or favoritism shown. The king was bound by his own law. So Daniel was arraigned before Darius. We could wish that all the conversation between the king and Daniel had been recorded, but the last words of Darius to Daniel are most moving, "Thy God whom thou servest continually, he will deliver thee." Verse 16.

Daniel Lowered to the Lions

With feigned loyalty the accusers lowered Daniel into the den of lions, closed the mouth of the pit with a stone, and saw to it that it was sealed with the king's seal, as well as that of his lords. That night Darius, in deep despondency, could not sleep. Nor would he tolerate any entertainment. He even refused food.

"The king arose very early in the morning, and went in haste unto the den of lions. And . . . he cried with a lamentable voice unto Daniel: . . . O Daniel, servant of the living God, is thy God, whom thou servest continually, able to deliver thee from the lions?" Verses 19, 20.

Daniel called back, "My God hath sent his angel, and hath shut the lions' mouths, that they have not hurt me." Verse 22.

The king's heart bounded with joy. Here was the answer not only to Daniel's prayer, but also to the prayers of Darius. When Daniel was taken up, not even a scratch was found upon him. Those wild, hungry cats had been under the control of a higher decree than that of an earthly king. An angel from God had been Daniel's companion all the long night. Perhaps the prayer of King David had been on his lips that night: "My soul is among the lions: and I lie even among them that are set on fire. . . . My heart is fixed, O God, my heart is fixed." Psalm 57:4, 7.

Did somebody suggest that the lions were not hungry? The next part of the story is almost too terrible to contemplate. Those men who had accused Daniel were thrown into the den and their families with them. The record says the lions tore them to pieces before they reached the bottom.

Darius Recognizes the God of Israel

The story of Daniel's deliverance became known throughout the land, for Darius sent a royal letter "to all people, nations, and languages, that dwell in all the earth." In this letter he gave his testimony to the living God who "delivereth and rescueth," declaring that He "worketh signs and wonders in heaven and in earth." What was to be the execution of one man became a bloodbath for his accusers. After the deliverance, the God of Israel was again proclaimed to the people throughout that vast empire. This was the third royal document that proceeded from the city of Babylon as a eulogy of the God of heaven. The first was sent by Nebuchadnezzar telling the story of the fiery furnace and the deliverance of the three Hebrews. The second was Nebuchadnezzar's portrayal of his insanity, recovery, and restoration. The third came from this Median king, and again it was a tribute to God's power to save those who trust in Him. The same God who delivered Daniel and his three companions is the God we serve today. If, while reading this, you feel that subtle intrigue surrounds your life, that there seems no way through, then let the example of these heroes of old inspire you to be true to the living God. He has a thousand ways to meet your need. Trust Him fully. He will bring you through. David said, "Mine enemies would daily swallow me up: for they be many that fight against me." But he then added, "What time I am afraid, I will trust in thee. . . . I will not fear what flesh can do unto me." Psalm 56:2-4. Isaiah was even more confident. He said, "I will trust, and not be afraid." Isaiah 12:2. Find your strength, dear friend, where these men found theirs. We can be more than conquerors through Christ Jesus our Lord.

This thrilling story of faith and victory finds us halfway through the book of Daniel. The first six chapters deal largely with history, the last six with prophecy. This latter section is without doubt the more fascinating part of the book. The visions Daniel received from the Lord cover the whole history of the world from his day to our own. In the earlier chapters, Daniel was heaven's ambassador at earthly courts. In the last chapters he is God's spokesman to the world, opening up the history of the future and especially that which affects the people of God.

In these chapters we will discover that the living God not only predicts what will happen but foretells the movements of men and nations hundreds, even thousands of years before the events. One of the impressive things about the book of Revelation, the last book of the Bible, is that it is really a commentary on the last six chapters of Daniel. Recognizing the importance of prophecy, let us turn to these chapters with reverence, praying that the Holy Spirit who moved Daniel to write these visions will guide us as we seek to comprehend God's last message of grace in these troublous days.

9
Cartoon Prophecies
of World Empires

One of the most comprehensive prophecies in all the Bible is found in Daniel, chapter 7, which portrays the rise, development, and collapse of human governments from Babylon to the end of the age—"until the times of the Gentiles be fulfilled." Luke 21:24.

God had revealed the succession of history's great empires nearly fifty years earlier, when Daniel had interpreted Nebuchadnezzar's dream. The Chaldean king had seen the future unfolded in the form of a metallic man. That vision has well been called the "ABC of apocalyptic prophecy." But later Daniel himself saw in vision the shape of things to come in the form of fierce beasts.

It was Belshazzar's first year when this vision appeared. Daniel 7:1. Nabonidus had made his son Belshazzar coregent of the empire in the year 553 B.C. Fourteen years before the festival when the Persian armies overthrew the city, the glory of the empire was already waning.

Nabonidus may have felt that bringing his eldest son into a place of rulership would strengthen the empire. Actually, this change in the leadership proved to be one of the reasons why Cyrus found the conquest of this great city comparatively easy. The father of Belshazzar, as we have already noticed, spent most of his time in the city of Tema in northern Arabia, being more interested in archaeology and history than in politics. He therefore left his son in charge of Babylon, in an administrative office for which Belshazzar was ill-prepared.

Now let us look at this great apocalyptic prophecy, noting how much more detail the Lord gave to Daniel than to Nebuchadnezzar. Apocalyptic prophecy is one of the most unique forms of literature, conveying its message in signs or symbols.

"I saw in my vision by night, and, behold, the four winds of the heaven strove upon the great sea. And four great beasts came up from the sea, diverse one from another. The first was like a lion, and had eagle's wings: I beheld till the wings thereof were plucked, and it was lifted up from the earth, and made stand upon the feet as a man, and a man's heart was given to it." Daniel 7:2-4. And in the following verses the prophet describes three more strange creatures.

What are we to understand by these great beasts? No need to use our imagination here, for the Bible is its own interpreter. Said the angel, "These great beasts, which are four, are four kings, which shall arise out of the earth." Verse 17. Verse 23 reads, "The fourth beast shall be the fourth kingdom upon earth." So these beasts are not four individual kings, but rather four successive kingdoms or world empires.

Interpreting the Language of Symbols

While symbolic language may appear bewildering at first, the meaning soon becomes clear and also fascinating. What are we to understand by the "winds" striving on the sea? Jeremiah, a contemporary of Daniel, prophecied: "The Lord hath a controversy with the nations . . . ; he will give them that are wicked to the sword. . . . A great whirlwind shall be raised up from the coasts of the earth." Jeremiah 25:31, 32. Wind in symbolic prophecy, therefore, is used to represent strife and war. But what does the "sea" represent? Isaiah indicates that water in prophecy symbolizes a multitude of people. Isaiah 17:12, 13. And in Revelation 17:15 we read: "The waters which thou sawest . . . are peoples, and multitudes, and nations, and tongues."

The beasts represent great kingdoms of empires. With the winds representing strife and war, the sea representing peoples and multitudes, and the beasts representing empires, we can put the picture together. Daniel saw a succession of world empires which arose and fell as the result of war. That has been the pattern of our world from the beginning of recorded history.

The same succession of empires, as was portrayed in Nebuchadnezzar's image, now appears as fierce beasts with many added details. Babylon is not just a head of gold but a lion with eagle's wings. The lion (king of beasts) and the eagle (king of birds) denote both strength and speed of conquest—a fitting symbol of Babylon under the rule of Nebuchadnezzar. In recent years archaeologists have unearthed a number of sculptured winged lions among the ruins of ancient Babylon. Daniel saw something strange happening to the lion however. The wings were plucked off, and a man's heart was given to it. Could anything better express the change that came into the Babylonian Empire before it collapsed? In English history we read of Richard the Lion-Hearted. King Richard was a lion-hearted man, full of courage and strength. But here we have a man-hearted lion.

Medo-Persia Replaces Babylon

The kingdom of Babylon was not to endure for long, for another kingdom, represented by a bear, was soon to arise. "And behold another beast, a second, like to a bear, and it raised up itself on one side, and it had three ribs in the mouth of it between the teeth of it: and they said thus unto it, Arise, devour much flesh." Daniel 7:5.

More ponderous, but strong and rapacious, the bear was a fitting symbol of Medo-Persia, corresponding to the silver kingdom of chapter 2. Something else important—the bear "raised up itself on one side." Verse 5. History records that the Persian element of this dual empire was much the stronger.

The "three ribs" between the teeth of the bear were also significant; also the words, "Arise, devour much flesh." Unlike Cyrus, the later kings of Persia were notably intolerant and cruel. Since the second century of the Christian era, the three ribs have been interpreted as Babylon, Lydia, and Egypt. These three kingdoms were not to last. Their humiliating defeat on the battlefield of Gaugamela (or Arbela) in 331 B.C. ushered in a new empire represented by the leopard with four heads and four wings. It was easy to understand the bronze of the metallic image as representing Greece, but what is symbolized by the four wings and the four heads? If the two wings of the eagle represented Babylon's speed of conquest, then these four wings would denote exceptional celerity of movement. This certainly was true of Grecia under Alexander. In the brief space of eight years he welded the Greek city-states into a universal power.

Born of royal blood, this son of Philip of Macedon was a pupil of the great philosopher Aristotle. Throughout his conquests, Alexander kept in touch with his mentor. In one lightning campaign following another, he quickly conquered most of the known world. But he could not conquer himself. He is said to have died of a fever at the age of thirty-three brought on by a drunken debauch. When asked on his deathbed to whom he would leave the kingdom, he replied, "To the strongest."

Twenty years of internal strife and civil war followed Alexander's death, until after the Battle of Ipsus in 301 B.C. four of his generals divided the empire among themselves. Lysimachus took the north with Thrace and part of Asia Minor. Cassander took the west including Macedonia and Athens. Seleucus took the east with most of Syria, Mesopotamia, and Persia, while Ptolemy took the south including Egypt and Palestine. The four heads of the leopard beast were indeed significant. These divisions, however, weakened the empire and paved the way for the rising power of Rome.

The Strange Ten-horned Beast

While every beast differed from the others, this fourth creature defied description. It was so hideous compared with the preceding creatures that the prophet received a second vision to describe it. The angel described this crushing power as "dreadful and terrible, and strong exceedingly; and it had great iron teeth: it devoured and brake in pieces, and stamped the residue with the feet of it; and it was diverse from all the beasts that were before it; and it had ten horns." Daniel 7:7.

The prophet was particularly eager to "know the truth of the fourth beast, which was diverse from all the others." With ferocious iron teeth and nails of brass, it would devour and break in pieces all before it and would stamp the residue with his feet; nothing could stand before his power.

This fourth beast unquestionably symbolized the empire of the Caesars. This power crucified our Lord and martyred the apostles. A high point during a "Roman Holiday" was the slaughter of Christians, either as burning torches in the Colosseum or as food for ravenous beasts. But what about the ten horns, and especially "that horn that had eyes, and the mouth that spake very great things"? Verse 20. The angel explained that the ten horns were "ten kings that shall arise: and another shall rise after them; and he shall be diverse from the first, and he shall subdue three kings." Verse 24. While the Roman Empire was strong, cruel, and crushing, it was not all bad. Besides its network of fine roads, which aided Christians in carrying the gospel to their world, Rome also developed comprehensive laws.

Roman Empire Divided

But the time came when the empire was divided. Weakened by warfare and barbarian invasions, it finally fell. Then the "little horn" pushed its way into leadership, uprooting three of the ten kingdoms. Several centuries later the "Holy Roman Empire" arose. While "neither holy, nor Roman, nor an empire," it held sway for a thousand years.

On occasion interpreters of prophecy have alleged that "at no period of Roman history was the empire composed of precisely ten kingdoms." However, it is well documented that the ten kingdoms appeared *after* the decline and fall of the empire of the Caesars. Gibbon, as well as other authoritative historians, make it clear that the ten kingdoms did indeed come into being after Rome's collapse. In his *Horae Apocalypticae,* Elliott lists these as Anglo-Saxons, Alemanni, Franks, Visigoths, Suevi, Burgundians, Bavarians, Heruli, Vandals, and Ostrogoths. (Some of these were known by other names at different times, and some other lists suggest various different kingdoms.)

The angel told Daniel that the little horn, "whose look was more stout than his fellows," would uproot three horns, or kingdoms. How completely this was fulfilled when the popes came to power! Three kingdoms were uprooted: the Heruli, the Vandals, and the Ostrogoths. And it was because they were Arians in their belief—that is, they did not recognize Christ as eternal, but claimed that He was created. In A.D. 493 the Heruli met their fate; in A.D. 534 the Vandals; and in A.D. 538 the Ostrogoths' power was broken, but they continued until A.D. 552.

Europe Dominated by the Church

The little horn, though small at first, became strong, "more stout than his fellows." Verse 20. This power "made war with the saints, and prevailed against them," as the angel said, and would continue until heaven's great judgment would settle his destiny and "take away his dominion." Verses 21, 26.

The papacy dominated Western Europe during the medieval centuries and later extended its control to the new lands of the Western Hemisphere. Not only did the angel describe this power in specific ways; he also showed what his work would be. This prophecy was well understood by the great Protestant Reformers of the sixteenth century. In fact, their interpretations of the prophecies of Daniel and Revelation led them to break from the apostate medieval church. They called the people back to the Bible, showing clearly from God's Word how the papacy fulfilled Daniel's prophecies. "He shall speak great words against the most High," said the angel, "and shall wear out the saints of the most High, and think to change times and laws: and they shall be given into his hand until a time and times and the dividing of time." Daniel 7:25.

Leaders such as Luther, Calvin, Knox, and Cranmer pointed to Daniel 7 and Revelation 17, identifying the great apostasy with headquarters in Rome. The Scriptural message of Revelation 18:4 formed the basis of many of their sermons, "Come out of her, my people, that ye be not partakers of her sins."

Powerful Preachers With a Mighty Message

These men were mighty preachers, and Paul's message in 2 Thessalonians 2:3, 4 concerning "that man of sin . . . who opposeth and exalteth himself above all that is called God, or that is worshipped," who "sitteth in the temple of God, shewing himself that he is God," moved the Reformers to action. They not only proclaimed the truth, but they were willing to die for it. And many did.

Some of the most brutal persecutions of all history, such as the Inquisition, were inspired by leaders of the church. The little-horn power did indeed wear out the saints of the most High. Millions of God's faithful men and women suffered martyrdom; many by fire, others by the sword, the ax, drowning, flaying, and the rack.

Changing God's Times and Laws

The angel further declared that this power would "think to change times and laws." Verse 25. Rome's attack on God's Ten Commandments is vital, but the changing of the "times" is also deeply significant. Great prophetic time prophecies relating to our Lord's first advent—His ministry, death, and resurrection—are clearly delineated in Daniel's prophecies. But these have been changed and reinterpreted, as we shall see in our next chapter. Also important prophecies concerning our Saviour's return, particularly those that focus on this apostate power, outlining its work, have been changed so that the great antichrist of the centuries has been disguised. (We shall consider this point in more detail when we come to the prophecy of Daniel 9.)

Not only would this power attempt to change the great chronological prophecies, the prophetic "times," but this power would even dare to lay his hand upon God's holy law. On this the Reformers were also very clear. Two commandments, particularly the second and the fourth, are clear evidences of this. The second commandment which forbids the making of graven images, in most Roman Catholic catechisms is attached to the first and reads: "I am the Lord thy God. Thou shall have no strange gods before me." This, of course, omits all reference to bowing to graven images.

Concerning the Sabbath commandment Luther said, "They allege the change of the Sabbath into the Lord's day, contrary, as it seemeth to the Decalogue; and they have no example more in their mouths than the change of the Sabbath. They will needs have the Church's power to be very great, because it hath dispensed with a precept of the Decalogue."—*Creeds of Christendom*, Volume 3, page 64.

One of the ablest of the Reformers, Philipp Melanchthon, a close associate of Luther, was even more specific. He said, "He changeth the tymes and lawes that any of the sixe work dayes commanded of God will make them unholy and idle dayes when he lyste, or of their own holy dayes abolished make work dayes again, or when they changed ye Saturday into Sonday."—*Exposicion of Daniel the Prophete* (gathered out of Philipp Melanchthon by George Joye, 1545.)

A Counterfeit Rest Day

Some years ago Dr. Edward T. Hiscox, a Baptist scholar and theologian who authored *The Baptist Manual*, addressed a large group of ministers in New York on this question. Concerning Sunday as a day of worship he said, "What a pity that it comes branded with the mark of paganism christened with the name of the sun god when adopted and sanctioned by the papal apostasy, and bequeathed as a sacred legacy to Protestantism." What a pity indeed! But this was all foretold in the prophecies of Daniel, Paul, and John. Eusebius, church historian in the time of Constantine, states it this way: "All things whatever it was our duty to do on the Sabbath, these we [the apostate church] have transferred to the Lord's day."—*Commentary on Psalm 92.*

These claims were later emphasized by the Counter-Reformation which grew out of the Council of Trent. This council was convened in an effort on the part of the papacy to meet the challenge of the Protestant Reformation. Note these words from the first session of that important council: "The celebration of the Sabbath should be transferred to the Lord's Day."—*Catechism of the Council of Trent.*

The angel also told how long this power was to be in control— "a time and times and the dividing of time." Daniel 7:25. A "time" was a year, "times" would be two years, and the dividing of time would be half a year (see Daniel 12:7), making a total of three and a half years. A Jewish year, recognized by Bible scholars, is 360 days, this being the mean average between a lunar year of 356 days and a solar year of 365 days. Let us add these figures together:

$$1 \text{ time} = 360 \text{ days}$$
$$2 \text{ times} = 720 \text{ days}$$
$$\tfrac{1}{2} \text{ times} = 180 \text{ days}$$
$$\overline{1,260 \text{ days}}$$

In symbolic prophecy a day may stand for a literal year, as in Ezekiel 4:6 and Numbers 14:34, "each day for a year." Then 1,260 prophetic days would be 1,260 literal years. This measurement of time is brought to view in Revelation 12:6, which reads "a thousand two hundred and threescore days." In Revelation 13:5 the same prophetic period is stated in a little different way, "forty and two months." A Jewish month is 30 days, so 42 multiplied by 30 brings the same total—1,260 days or years. In Revelation 12:14 the same period is differently stated: "a time, and times, and half a time." In the year A.D. 538 the rule of the Ostrogoths was definitely broken, leaving the papacy free to develop her political and ecclesiastical power. This she did, and for 1,260 years she exercised great authority in Europe, crowning kings and deposing them.

The Reformers Challenge the Church

The Protestant Reformers of the sixteenth and seventeenth centuries challenged the church's power, but by 1798 papal power in Europe had severely weakened. That year, in the Napoleonic Wars, Pope Pius VI was taken prisoner in Rome by General Berthier of France. He died in exile a year and a half later. From A.D. 538 to A.D. 1798 is, we repeat, 1,260 years.

The arrest of Pope Pius made dramatic news. Many Protestants recognizing in the arrest the fulfillment of prophecies of Daniel and Revelation, felt that the event both confirmed the truths they had proclaimed and inspired an intensive study of the prophecies. Especially they studied the eschatological prophecies—those relating to the second advent of our Lord. The result was a great spiritual awakening in Europe, in the Middle East, in India, in North and South America, even as far away as the new land of Australia.

The words of the angel, "the judgment shall sit, and they shall take away his dominion, to consume and to destroy it unto the end," came with new meaning. "The kingdom and dominion, and the greatness of the kingdom under the whole heaven, shall be given to the people of the saints of the most High, whose kingdom is an everlasting kingdom, and all dominions shall serve and obey him. Hitherto is the end of the matter." Daniel 7:26-28. This could mean nothing more or less than the end of the age, which would be ushered in by the second advent of Christ.

The "Advent Awakening" Is Born

The reaction was tremendous. With new confidence men and women by hundreds of thousands pored over the prophecies. This was the prelude to the "Great Advent Awakening."

When the angel came to the climax of his message, Daniel was speechless. But he says, "I kept the matter in my heart." Verse 28.

Are we stirred by this revelation? Does the knowledge of the Lord's return sober us and inspire us? The prophecy reveals that no other world empire will arise until our Lord returns. What courage that should bring to our hearts! While definite attempts are being made today to establish a new world order, we can know that if such a world government were to be established it would be short-lived.

The next great event on this planet will be the ushering in of the eternal kingdom of glory. And that kingdom will be established not by human councils and legislation but by our Lord Himself. What a contrast it will be from all the kingdoms of the past and the present. It will be a kingdom of peace and love—no armies, no navies, no police, no prisons. Riots, demonstrations, poverty, and hunger will be no more. The citizens of that kingdom shall never say, "I am sick," for pain and death will be banished forever.

This is the kingdom for which God's people through all the ages have waited and prayed. Are you, dear friend, a citizen of God's kingdom of grace now? If you are, you will also be a citizen of the kingdom of glory then. Christ loved us so much that He died in our place, so that you and I might live with Him eternally. Not only did He die, He rose again and ascended to His Father's throne from whence He sends forth His Spirit to deliver us from sin and rebellion and make us members of His family.

Each of us must make a decision individually. Jesus said, "He that is not with me is against me." As we close this chapter, we simply ask, are you with Him or against Him?

10
Antichrist and
Heaven's Judgment

Scripture refers to God's great judgment more than a thousand times. Almost every Bible writer makes some reference to it. But no more sublime description is given than in Daniel 7:9-14. The nature of the scene demands our serious consideration. The expression "thrones were cast down" is unfortunate. "Thrones were placed" is more correct, as the Revised Standard Version translates the text. Daniel was given a vision of the coming judgment when "the Ancient of days" would take his place, surrounded by a group sitting on lesser thrones. Ten thousand times ten thousand angels, plus thousands more, joined the scene. The prophet John describes the same scene in Revelation 5:11: "I beheld, and I heard the voice of many angels round about the throne . . . : and the number of them was ten thousand times ten thousand, and thousands of thousands."

We usually think of the judgment as a scene with a judge, a prisoner in the dock, and a defense attorney pleading his case. However, a judgment scene in the days of John was quite different. When one who was to preside took his place, then a group of associates took their places in a semicircle. These were special seats, or judgment thrones, and those who occupied those places were representatives. An interesting allusion to this is found in Psalm 122:1-5, where the psalmist says, "I was glad when they said unto me, Let us go into the house of the Lord." Then he goes on to tell about some things he finds here. Berkeley's version of verse 5 reads, "For here seats are placed for judging."

97

Daniel was given a view of the Ancient of Days, God the Father, taking His place. It is He who *presides* in the judgment. Then in verse 13 the Son of man appears to *perform* the work. This is sometimes called the investigative judgment because there the evidence is presented. A more illuminating title would be the preadvent judgment, for this takes place before the Son of man returns for His people. And the prophecy says that earthly powers are still struggling for supremacy while this judgment is in session. When our Lord returns in glory, He brings His rewards with Him (Revelation 22:12)—a statement which indicates that the destiny of every soul will have been settled before the second advent. In this preadvent judgment, the God of the universe will give a full account of His work in the salvation of men. He will uncover the sinister influences of Lucifer, who has charged God with being unjust.

(Sin did not begin on earth. In heaven the highest of the angels led a rebellion against God. He said, "I will exalt my throne above the stars of God: I will sit also upon the mount of the congregation, in the sides of the north: I will ascend above the heights of the clouds; I will be like the most High." Isaiah 14:13, 14. When Lucifer challenged God's rulership, one third of the heavenly hosts joined in that rebellion, and they were all cast out of heaven. Revelation 12:4, 7-9.)

God Vindicated in the Judgment

The judgment Daniel describes in verses 9 and 10 of Daniel 7 is the same as that of Revelation 14:7. The central issue in the judgment is the vindication of the character of God before the whole universe. Thus it is called "The hour of God's judgment." Part of that judgment will be the presentation of the records. This is the crisis hour of the universe, when God puts himself on trial.

"When thou speakest thou shalt be vindicated, and win the verdict when thou art on trial." Romans 3:4, NEB. Not only are *we* on trial, but God Himself is on trial. He planned it that way so that the whole universe can study the story of sin and finally participate in the vindication of His character. When that judgment ends, every creature in the universe will stand on one side or the other of the issue. The Bible does not teach that all will be saved, but it does teach that "we must all appear before the judgment seat of Christ;

that every one may receive the things done in his body, according to that he hath done, whether it be good or bad." 2 Corinthians 5:10. When God uncovers all the records,. He will reveal to the universe not only His patience and forgiving love, but also who of the human family will have accepted His grace and therefore be candidates for immortality, which will be bestowed on the righteous at the second advent of our Lord.

God, of course, does not have to study record books to discover who will be saved. "The Lord knoweth them that are his." 2 Timothy 2:19. But the judgment reveals God's justice and mercy to the universe.

At the conclusion of that heavenly assize the Son of man comes before the Ancient of Days, God the Father. Then "there was given him dominion, and glory, and a kingdom, that all people, nations, and languages, should serve him: his dominion is an everlasting dominion, which shall not pass away, and his kingdom that which shall not be destroyed." Daniel 7:14.

Our Representative in the Judgment

The coming of the Son of man before the Ancient of Days is full of meaning, and the term "Son of man" is also significant. Some translations read "one human in form," emphasizing His humanity. As repentant sinners we have a representative, one like ourselves, before the Father. Jesus evidently took this term "Son of man" from the seventh chapter of Daniel, and the New Testament records more than eighty occasions when He used it.

He concludes His ministry of reconcilation by this work of judgment. While He is our advocate, he is also our judge. Christ Himself said, "The Father judgeth no man, but hath committed all judgment unto the Son. . . . and hath given him authority to execute judgment also, because he is the Son of man." John 5:22, 27.

While it is the Father who *presides* in this august assembly as the Ancient of Days, yet it is the Son who *performs* the judgment. (See *The Great Controversy*, pages 479, 480.) God has "appointed a day, in the which he will judge the world in righteousness by that man whom he hath ordained; whereof he hath given assurance unto all men, in that he hath raised him from the dead." Acts 17:31. This can be none other than Jesus Christ.

Christ, Our Judge

Note these important words in *The Desire of Ages*, page 210: "It is He who has encountered the deceiver, and who through all the ages has been seeking to wrest the captives from his grasp, who will pass judgment upon every soul." The same author has written: "Christ Himself will decide who are worthy to dwell with the family of heaven. He will judge every man according to his words and his works."—*Christ's Object Lessons*, page 74. And again: "Christ has been made our Judge. The Father is not the Judge. The angels are not. He who took humanity upon Himself, and in this world lived a perfect life, is to judge us. He only can be our Judge. Will you remember this, brethren? Will you remember it, ministers? Will you remember it, fathers and mothers? Christ took humanity that He might be our Judge."—Ellen G. White, *Testimonies*, Vol. 9, p. 185.

It was our Lord Himself who said, "The Father . . . hath committed all judgment unto the Son." This refers not only to the preadvent judgment but also to the pronouncement of the sentence and the execution of that sentence.

At the very time that the preadvent judgment is in session, the "little horn" power, which we noticed in the previous chapter, is heard to speak "great words against the most High," uttering his most blasphemous claims. An even clearer picture of what that means to us is presented in Daniel 8, which deals particularly with the sanctuary and God's provisions of salvation for sinners.

To understand the messages of Daniel fully we must understand something of the Hebrew sanctuary, for the prophecy declared that the truths of that sanctuary would be "cast down . . . to the ground" and trodden under foot. Daniel 8:10, 11.

How and when was all this to happen? This eighth chapter could well be called the key to understanding Daniel. In this chapter we are introduced to a most important vision of a ram, a goat, and a little-horn power that would seek to destroy the truths of salvation. This vision was given to Daniel two years after the vision of the great beasts recorded in chapter 7. That vision came in "the first year of king Belshazzar," but the events of chapter 8 were brought to Daniel's notice "in the third year of his reign." The prophet received this vision when he was at Shushan in the province of Elam, or Elymias, in Persia. This was a mountainous region occupied originally by a Cushite race. In Genesis 14, we read of Chedorlaomer who founded an extensive empire including Elam, which, according to some historians, became independent as early as 2280 B.C. Later Elam's king attacked Babylon, transporting many spoils to Shushan, or Susa, including the famous code of Hammurabi. Susa lay on the direct route from Babylon to India.

In Danel's day there was evidently a large canal which connected the two rivers, the Coprates and the Choaspes. The canal was called Eluacus or Ulai. Daniel was probably on official business for Babylon when God gave him this very important vision. He says, "I lifted up mine eyes, and saw, and, behold, there stood before the river a ram which had two horns: and the two horns were high; but one was higher than the other, and the higher came up last. I saw the ram pushing westward, and northward, and southward; so that no beasts might stand before him, neither was there any that could deliver out of his hand; but he did according to his will, and became great." Daniel 8:3, 4.

Gabriel Interprets the Symbols

There is no need to guess concerning the interpretation of this vision, for the angel Gabriel made it very clear: "The ram which thou sawest having two horns are the kings of Media and Persia." Daniel 8:20. Under Cyrus the Great, Persia became the stronger force in the dual kingdom, the "higher horn" coming up last. The ram was the symbol of Persia at that time, just as the lion today represents Britain. In fact, the Persian kings were crowned with a ram's head of gold, jeweled with precious stones. Moreover their coins carried the figure of a ram. In this prophecy the ram pushed westward, taking Babylonia, Mesopotamia, and Syria; northward taking Armenia and the area of the Caspian Sea; and southward, engulfing Egypt, the Holy Land, Libya, and Ethiopia.

"No beasts [powers] might stand before him." The advance of the Medo-Persian Empire was overwhelming. Then the prophet said, "As I was considering, behold, an he goat came from the west on the face of the whole earth, and touched not the ground: and the goat had a notable horn between his eyes." Daniel 8:5.

Gabriel interpreted this symbol: "And the rough goat is the king of Grecia: and the great horn that is between his eyes is the first king." Verse 21. That king, of course, was Alexander the Great, who in a little less than a decade conquered the ancient world. The goat king in the prophecy "came from the west . . . , and touched not the ground." Conquering Asia Minor, Syria, Phoenicia, Cyprus, Egypt, Babylonia, Persia, and the mountains north of India, he took his troops as far east as the Indus River. But the soldiers, having been away from home more than seven years, forced Alexander to return. He traveled as far back as Babylon, where he intended to make his headquarters. But mourning the loss of a favorite friend, it is reported he was seized by a sudden illness ("swamp fever"), perhaps malaria, which was complicated by heavy drinking. Though only 33 years old, he died in a few days. This conquering genius left a military record rarely if ever surpassed. How true is the prophecy!

The symbol of Greece was the goat. Tradition has it that Caremus the first king of Macedon followed a herd of wild goats to Edessa, where he set up his capital, calling it Aege, "the goat city," from whence the national symbol sprang. The prophecy indicated a dramatic change—"when he was strong, the great horn was broken." In its place four horns appeared. It is said that when Alexander lay dying, Perdiccas, his faithful friend, asked to whom he would leave the kingdom. He replied, "To the strongest." Upon his decease, the empire was thrown into a state of strife until it was completely broken. The army scattered, and the cities were plundered. At last four of Alexander's generals divided the empire between them as noted earlier. Lysimachus took the north, including Cappadocia, Thrace, and northern Asia Minor. Ptolemy took the south—Egypt, Cyprus, and Palestine. Cassander claimed Macedonia, Thessaly and Greece. Seleucus took the east, including Babylonia, Persia, and Syria.

Note carefully the language in the rest of the prophecy, because there is perhaps more confusion on this than on any other part of the book. Scripture says, "And out of one of them came forth a little horn, which waxed exceeding great, toward the south, and toward the east, and toward the pleasant land. And it waxed great, even to the host of heaven." Verses 9, 10.

Then, he "shall destroy the mighty and the holy people," and "he shall also stand up against the Prince of princes." Verses 24, 25.

Many commentators see in these verses a description of Antiochus Epiphanes, eighth king in the Seleucid dynasty. While this man certainly was a tyrant and a persecutor, having done all he could against the Jews, yet he certainly was not this little-horn power described in the text. True, he profaned the temple in Jerusalem by sacrificing a sow at the altar of burnt offering and then sprinkling its broth over the temple walls. And while doing all that, he tried to enforce the worship of Olympus and massacred more than 100,000 Jews who refused such idolatrous worship. Because of his frightful acts of sacrilege, he was despised not only by the Jews but also by his own people. However, Antiochus was only one of a line of kings and by no means the strongest. When we have said the worst we could about him, he comes short of the prophetic description.

Who Was the "Exceeding Great" Power?

Note these important points—the ram representing Persia was to become "great"; the goat representing Greece was to become "very great." But this new power symbolized by the little horn was to become "exceeding great." Surely neither Antiochus Epiphanes nor any other of his line was greater than Cyrus or Alexander. Actually, Antiochus was anything but great. He was forced to pay tribute to Rome constantly; he was killed trying to raise more money to pay tribute. It would be hard to find in history a ruler that was more eccentric. Today we might call him paranoid. Even his own people sometimes referred to him as Antiochus Epimanes "the madman." He did not enlarge his territory. He was simply one among many kings. If it were left to historians alone to select a man to fill the role, it certainly would not be Antiochus Epiphanes. The choice of this man is part of a design to shift the focus from the power clearly indicated. And we do well to probe this.

The prophecy says, "Out of one of them came forth a little horn, which waxed exceeding great, toward the south, and toward the east, and toward the pleasant land. And it waxed great, even to the host of heaven. . . . Yea, he magnified himself even to the prince of the host." Verses 9-11.

The power introduced here was to do things Antiochus Epiphanes could never do. How could Antiochus stand up against the Prince of princes, when the former died in 164 B.C., long before our Lord was born? Some suggest that Antiochus was only a type of a greater power—the antichrist—who will appear in the end time. The real fulfillment, they say, lies in the future, after Christ's second advent. But what right does anyone have to throw this prophecy off into the future (as do many interpreters of prophecy) when the Scripture indicates no such gap?

Note carefully: This new power was to come "out of one of them" that is, out of one of the four divisions of the Grecian Empire. It would be small at the beginning but would wax "exceeding great" toward the south (the Egyptian kingdom) and toward the east (the Seleucid kingdom) and toward the pleasant land (Palestine). The kingdom which Antiochus ruled was already in the east. It could not, therefore, refer to him. It must be some other power. We must then look for a power greater than Persia or Greece. Only one fulfills the prophecy, and that is Rome, the fourth in the succession of empires. Egypt was made a province of Rome in 30 B.C. Rome had conquered Syria some years earlier in 65 B.C., and in 63 B.C. Palestine was incorporated into the Roman Empire. More than a century later the wrath of Rome fell upon the Jews with great violence. In response to untold provocations, Rome's armies marched against Jerusalem in A.D. 66, and the war dragged on for four years. Finally in A.D. 70 the legions under the command of Titus stormed the walls. They completely destroyed the city and the temple and scattered the Jews throughout the empire.

Rome was graphically portrayed as the "iron kingdom" in chapter 2 and also as the indescribable beast with ten horns in chapter 7. Chapter 8 portrays this power also and gives many more details. The Roman Empire bitterly persecuted both the Jewish nation and the Christian church, having previously ordered the crucifixion of an innocent man, Christ Jesus. But the Iron Empire was not to last forever. It broke up into ten kingdoms, and another power moved in to take its place. In the previous chapter we noticed that the little-horn power pushed its way into the forefront, uprooting three of the ten kingdoms. It was not merely the political power, but the religious power, the apostate church, that is portrayed in Daniel, chapters 7 and 8.

Ecclesiastical Rome Corrupts the Gospel

To grasp the full meaning of Daniel 8:11, we need to realize that the word "sacrifice" is not in the original text. It was supplied by the translators. The word translated "daily" is from the Hebrew *tamid*, which occurs 103 times in the Old Testament. It means "continual" or "continually," and is used generally in connection with the ancient sanctuary services such as the "continual burnt offering," "continual shewbread," "continual incense," et cetera. These services foreshadowed the continual mediation of our Lord on behalf of sinners. For hundreds of years a priestly ministry was carried out in the Mosaic sanctuary. Later it was continued in the temple.

The burnt offering foreshadowed our Lord's death on the cross as the Lamb of God; the shewbread and the incense were types of His ministry as High Priest and Intercessor in the heavenly sanctuary. Hebrews 7:3; 4:15; 8:1, 2; 9:11, 12. The prophecy in Daniel revealed that these central truths of the gospel would be cast down to the ground and stamped upon. Even, "the place of his sanctuary was cast down." This happened first when Rome destroyed Jerusalem and erected a temple to Jupiter on the temple's former site.

The Emperor Joins the Church

Two and a half centuries later the apostate church had become so popular that the Emperor Constantine became a nominal Christian and, just prior to his death, a baptized member. Soon bishops became government officers, carrying out the dictates of the state. State officials were also appointed to high positions in the church, irrespective of their qualifications either morally or spiritually. This not only corrupted the church but paved the way for the introduction of pagan practices into the worship services. Little by little the gospel of salvation by grace alone was buried beneath a plethora of ceremonies, rituals, and penances.

In A.D. 800 Charlemagne, king of the Franks, created the "Holy Roman Empire" in which the church joined the state in many areas. Those were dark days for true Christianity and also for the Jews, who were forced into ghettos with no civil rights and little justice. The light of truth in many places was almost obliterated. Moffatt's translation of verse 11 reads, "It even magnified itself to match the

Prince of the starry host, and deprived him of the daily sacrifice."

In rabbinical literature the "daily" included the evening and morning sacrifices which became "the center and core of public worship."—Dr. J. A. Herts, *The Pentateuch and Hoftorahs*, page 694.

These sacrifices were designated by *tamid*, translated "daily" in the English. We have already noticed that this word stood for the continual manifestation of Christ at the throne of grace. But the prophecy tells how this new power would "magnify himself" and "prosper, and practise" corrupting the gospel and taking glory from the "prince of the host."

Instead of the pure gospel centering in the finished sacrifice of Christ on Calvary, now ministering as our High Priest in the heavenly sanctuary, a false gospel insinuated itself. This centered in an earthly sanctuary with headquarters in Rome and manned by an earthly priesthood. No matter how sincere these priests may be, the church has declared that "Christ is offered on our altars every day." In Faber's *Catechism for the Catholic Parochial Schools*, page 72, ‡359, we read: "Question: Is the sacrifice of Christ on the cross still offered? Answer: The sacrifice of Christ on the cross is still offered in every mass."

While not questioning the sincerity of our Roman Catholic friends, we would point out that the very heart of the New Testament message is that Jesus Christ has been offered "once for all" on the cross. And by virtue of that finished sacrifice, He is now at the throne of grace ministering for us. The system of an earthly priesthood and the sacrifice of the mass is really alien to the gospel of Christ. Through the mass, the confessional, and the doctrine of salvation by works, this religious system has indeed "cast down the truth to the ground."

How Long Until the Sanctuary Truth Would Be Proclaimed?

While Daniel was watching the activities of the little horn, he heard a dialogue between two heavenly beings. A question was asked, "For how long shall be the period the vision shall last? . . . How long will impiety cause desolation?" Verse 13, NEB. The answer came, "And he said unto me, Unto two thousand and three hundred days; then shall the sanctuary be cleansed." The Hebrew word here translated "cleansed" means "justified" or "made right." A volume could be written on this statement. "The justification of the sanctuary is the vindication of its cause," says A. Bevan, "for as long as it is polluted it lies under condemnation."—*A Short Commentary on the Book of Daniel.*

This period of 2,300 days has presented a real challenge to commentators. Some suggest that *ereb boqer,* translated "days," should read "evenings and mornings" as in the Revised Standard Version. Therefore, they say it is only 1,150 actual days. To this Keil replies: "A Hebrew reader could not possibly understand the period of 2,300 evenings and mornings as 2300 half days or 1150 whole days, because evening and morning at creation consisted not of half days but of whole days."—*The Book of the Prophet Daniel,* quoted in *The Prophecy of Daniel,* Edward J. Young, page 174.

The time period in this vision is very specific, but at this point the precise time for the beginning was not indicated. Daniel was naturally concerned and sought earnestly for the meaning. Gabriel was then told to make the matter clear to Daniel. He informed the prophet that the vision belonged to "the time of the end." Verse 17. And "at the time appointed the end shall be." Verse 19.

"The period determined was long." Dr. Bung, a Jewish writer, declares the prophet understood the expression "then shall the sanctuary be cleansed," for that occurred every year on the Day of Atonement, "the tenth day of the seventh month." When he received this vision, the sanctuary and the holy city of Jerusalem had already been destroyed by the Babylonians. Even had the temple been standing, the long period of 2,300 days could not be fitted into the regular pattern; and being a prophetic period, the days represented actual years. No wonder Gabriel said: "Shut thou up the vision; for it shall be for many days." Verse 26. "It is far distant," as Fenton translates it.

The angel's explanation of all that was to happen proved too much for the aging prophet. He fainted and was sick for a time. When he recovered, he carried out his governmental responsibilities. But neither he nor any of his associates could understand the vision. The symbols of the ram and the goat were clear; the angel had explained that portion of the vision. But concerning the "sanctuary and the host" and the power that would stand up against the

"Prince of princes," as well as the long period of 2,300 days, these concerned the prophet greatly but none understood it.

Daniel Receives the Explanation

Considerable time elapsed between the receiving of this vision and its interpretation. Not until the overthrow of the Babylonian Empire some years later did Daniel receive the explanation of those points. Sometimes we get impatient for God's answer to our problems, but let us remember that even Daniel, a prophet and a man greatly beloved of God, had to wait years for God's answer.

The explanation of the vision we find in the next chapter, Daniel 9, verses 21-27. This is the most precise outline prophecy in the Bible. It provides the master key to the correct understanding of our Lord's first advent and the conditions leading to His second advent. We will note this in detail in our next chapter.

Before leaving chapter 8, we should note that the 2,300-days prophecy of Daniel 8:14 seems to have been given by Christ Himself, called in the marginal reference (in some KJV Bibles) of verse 13 "the numberer of secrets, or the wonderful numberer." In Isaiah 9:6, He is called "Wonderful, Counselor, The mighty God, The everlasting Father, The Prince of peace." The description of Daniel 10:5, 6 is repeated in Revelation 1:13-16. So important is this prophecy concerning the cleansing of the sanctuary that it was not left for lesser beings to describe. It came to the prophet from the One who is "the Judge of all the earth." But even His truth would be attacked by the one described as of "fierce countenance, and understanding dark sentences," (verse 23) whom the angel said would "magnify himself" (verse 25) and "destroy the mighty and the holy people" (verse 24).

To clash between the Prince of princes and this corrupting power would reach its climax in the teachings and work of the antichrist, and this would happen prior to the second advent of our Lord. In this context Jesus urged His people to study the prophecies of Daniel. Tragic as this hour of history is, it is nevertheless full of wonderful meaning for those with eyes to see and ears to hear— those anointed by the Holy Spirit to discern the signs of the times. This generation is destined to witness tremendous things in the near future. Are we ready?

11
Daniel's Key Theme—The Sanctuary and Salvation

We now come to what may be considered the most important chapter in Daniel's unique book. Chapter 9 contains one of the greatest prophecies in the Bible. It opens up areas concerning the Messiah, His matchless ministry, His vicarious death, and His subsequent ministry as our High Priest at the throne of grace.

This marvelous revelation came in direct answer to the prophet's importunate prayer recorded in Daniel 9:4-19. Daniel tells us that he had been studying the books of Jeremiah and was greatly concerned about the fulfillment of the prophecy of seventy years of captivity. See Jeremiah 25:9, 11. He also found predictions in the writings of Isaiah concerning events at the close of the seventy years. The more the prophet pondered the writings of these prophets, the greater the sin of Israel appeared. In calculating the seventy years' captivity prophesied by Jeremiah, Daniel realized that the time had almost expired. Did he just let things take their course? No. He took the whole situation on his heart and gave himself to earnest intercessory prayer. With deep concern for his people he unburdened his soul to God.

Daniel's Moving Prayer

In humiliation and confession, this statesman-prophet, this confidant of kings, poured out his petitions in one of the greatest prayers ever recorded. This was no ordinary supplication; it was sacrificial prayer. He tells how he garbed himself in sackcloth, sprinkling ashes on his head, thus bearing the marks of mourning. "I prayed," he says, "and made my confession." What did this man of God have to confess? It was not his sin that brought the Jews into slavery. But as a true intercessor he made the nation's guilt his own.

Addressing Jehovah as the covenant-keeping God, he says, "*We* have sinned: . . . neither have *we* hearkened unto thy servants the prophets. . . . O Lord, righteousness belongeth unto thee, but unto *us* confusion of faces. . . . To the Lord our God belong mercies and forgivenesses, though *we* have rebelled against him; neither have *we* obeyed." Verses 5-10. He continues in the same vein: "For *our* sins, and for the iniquities of our fathers, Jerusalem and thy people are become a reproach to all that are about *us*. Now therefore, O our God, hear the prayer of thy servant, . . . and cause thy face to shine upon thy sanctuary." Verses 16, 17.

Some of his expressions he gathered from the Psalms: "Cause thy face to shine; and we shall be saved." Psalm 80:3, 7, 19. Also Aaron's priestly benediction contains this expression: "The Lord make his face to shine upon thee." Numbers 6:25.

With these thoughts in mind, Daniel pleads with Jehovah to cause His face to shine on His sanctuary. The temple, of course, had been destroyed long years before, but the time had come for it to be rebuilt. For the Lord's sake, Daniel presented his petition. As a true intercessor, Daniel, who for almost seventy years had been Heaven's ambassador in an alien land, says, "O Lord, hear; O Lord, forgive; O Lord, hearken and do." Such intense earnestness should stir the heart of every Christian, leading us to ask ourselves, Are we as concerned in our petitions as was this man of God? Are our prayers earnest intercessions, or are they mere formalities by reason of habit? The prophet's greatest concern was for the honor and reputation of Jehovah.

Gabriel Appears While Daniel Prays

"And whiles I was speaking, and praying, and confessing my sin and the sin of my people," said the prophet, "even the man Gabriel, whom I had seen in the vision at the beginning, being caused to fly swiftly, touched me about the time of the evening oblation." Verses 20, 21. Although the temple no longer existed, and the Levitical ritual had long since ceased, yet the prophet, believing the promise of God concerning the return of His people to Jerusalem and the restoration of the temple worship, made his prayer at the time of the evening sacrifice, about three o'clock in the afternoon.

In answer to Daniel's petition Gabriel made haste to be at the prophet's side. He came to give special instruction concerning "the vision" which he had seen a few years earlier. At that time no one, not even Daniel himself, understood it. So Gabriel began by saying "I am come to shew thee; . . . therefore understand the matter, and consider the vision." Verse 23. Then to make the matter clear, he introduced another prophecy concerning Daniel's people—the Jews —and especially the coming Messiah. He said, "Seventy weeks are determined upon thy people and upon thy holy city, to finish the transgression, and to make an end of sins, and to make reconciliation for iniquity, and to bring in everlasting righteousness, and to seal up the vision and prophecy, and to anoint the most Holy." Daniel 9:24.

Newer versions such as the Revised Standard and James Moffatt's are more exact in their translations: "anoint a most holy place"; "consecrate a most sacred Place." The consecration of this sacred place was without doubt the heavenly sanctuary, where the Messiah would officiate after giving His life as a sacrifice for us. And to confirm the promise, six tremendous events were to happen, all of them bound up with the Messiah. These were to be fulfilled during the last week of the seventy weeks.

In chapter 7 we noticed the prophetic period time, times, and a half, or 1,260 days. We also discovered that when we deal with prophetic time, a day stands for a literal year. See Numbers 14:34 and Ezekiel 4:6. These seventy weeks, then, would be weeks of years, a total of 490 years. Moreover, this period would be separated into three parts: 7 prophetic weeks, 49 years, allotted for the rebuilding of the city; 62 weeks, or 434 years, reach to "Messiah the Prince"; and one final week. These are vital measurements, but we must be certain when these 70 weeks begin. On this point Gabriel was emphatic, giving the event which would mark the beginning. He said it would be "from the going forth of the commandment to restore and to build Jerusalem." Verse 25.

Daniel did not live to see the issuance of that third decree, authorizing the rebuilding of the city. He did see the result of the first decree, by King Cyrus in 536 B.C., allowing the Jews to return to their homeland and rebuild their temple. Opposition from the

Samaritans, however, hindered the work on the temple, making necessary another decree by Darius Hystaspes in 519 B.C.

The Legal Language of the Decrees

The first proclamation which Cyrus put in writing reads: "The Lord God of heaven hath given me all the kingdoms of the earth; and he hath charged me to build him an house at Jerusalem, which is in Judah. Who is there among you of all his people? his God be with him, and let him go up to Jerusalem, which is in Judah, and build the house of the Lord God of Israel." Ezra 1:2, 3.

Seventeen years later Darius made a second proclamation, which was really a confirmation of that issued by King Cyrus. Darius' decree reads, "I make a decree what ye shall do to the elders of these Jews for the building of the house of God: that the king's goods . . . forthwith expenses be given unto these men, that they be not hindered." Ezra 6:8.

We emphasize again that, wonderful as these decrees were, they concerned only the reconstruction of the *temple,* the "house at Jerusalem." Another decree was issued by Artaxerxes Longimanus in 457 B.C., sixty-two years after that of Darius. This third decree authorized further rebuilding and restoration, the temple having been finished fifty-eight years earlier, in 515 BC. See Ezra 6:15.

Artaxerxes in his decree gave in effect a blank check to Ezra. Note again the language: "Artaxerxes, king of kings, unto Ezra the priest, a scribe of the law of the God of heaven. . . . I make a decree, that all they of the people of Israel . . . which are minded of their own freewill to go up to Jerusalem, go with thee." "And I, even I Artaxerxes the king, do make a decree to all the treasurers which are beyond the river, that whatsoever Ezra the priest . . . shall require of you, it be done speedily." Ezra 7:12, 13, 21.

Full Autonomy Given the Jews

This third decree included more than the restoration of the city, as verses 24-26 show. It gave the Jews as a nation autonomy in the matter of legal judgments, even to the death penalty if necessary. Verses 25, 26. The restoration of Jerusalem meant not merely the laying of stones and bricks, but the establishment of a nation with headquarters in the rebuilt city of Jerusalem.

It was the decree of Artaxerxes that gave the Jews their political existence. Many Jews had already returned as pilgrims and so-journers, but this last decree changed the situation, giving us the *terminus a quo.* The commencement of the seventy weeks prophecy was 457 B.C., which date is now accepted by many scholars (see *The Chronology of Ezra 7* by S. H. Horn and L. H. Wood).

Thirteen years later, in 444 B.C., Nehemiah, the king's cupbearer, was granted special permission to go to Jerusalem to join with and encourage the builders. Nehemiah accomplished a wonderful work in a very short time. But he was on leave of absence from the king; this was not a decree, and the permit was granted thirteen years after the royal decree for the rebuilding of the city had been issued. The Scriptures show that the temple had been completed about seventy years before Nehemiah's visit. In Ezra 6:14, 15 we read, "The elders of the Jews builded, and they prospered through the prophesying of Haggai the prophet and Zechariah the son of Iddo. . . . And this house [the temple] was finished on the third day of the month Adar, which was in the sixth year of the reign of Darius the king." This was the year 515 B.C. Artaxerxes' decree made pro-vision for the services of the temple, but it did not provide for the building of the temple.

Artaxerxes' Decree Issued for Ezra, Not Nehemiah

We repeat that the decree or commandment from Artaxerxes was given, not in 445 or 444, but in 457 B.C. This is the date for the beginning of the seventy weeks prophecy or the 490 years. It is unfortunate that so many Bible teachers take 445 or 444 B.C. for the date of the decree, when no decree was given then, nor was it needed, for it had been issued and put into effect thirteen years earlier.

Now note Gabriel's message to Daniel: "Seventy weeks are deter-mined upon thy people." The word "determined," *chathak* in Hebrew, has been variously translated as "decreed," "divided," "shortened," "fixed," "cut off," "cut short," "apportioned," and "al-lotted." These variations are significant. Seventy prophetic weeks were allotted to the Jews, during which certain definite things were to happen. The period of time was "cut off" or "shortened" from the longer period of the 2,300 prophetic days (literal years) of chapter

8, which the prophet said no one understood. Now Gabriel tells Daniel he has come to give him special instruction concerning the previous "vision," saying: "Know therefore and understand, that from the going forth of the commandment to restore and to build Jerusalem unto the Messiah the Prince shall be seven weeks, and threescore and two weeks: the street shall be built again, and the wall, even in troublous times." Verse 25.

The Temple Is Finished

The seven-week (forty-nine year) period, reaching to 408 B.C., was specified by the angel Gabriel, but present archaeological evidence has not revealed its full significance.

The period of sixty-nine prophetic weeks, 483 actual years, brings us to the year A.D. 27. Now what should we expect at that time? The prophecy says "unto Messiah the Prince." Did He appear then? Yes. The word Messiah means "anointed," and the Scripture says, "God anointed Jesus of Nazareth with the Holy Ghost and with power: who went about doing good, and healing all that were oppressed." Acts 10:38. But when was Jesus anointed? Not at His birth. He was Spirit-born, but not Spirit-baptized until He went to John, who baptized Him in the Jordan River.

Christ Baptized and Spirit-anointed

In Luke 3:21, 22 we read, "Now when all the people were baptized, it came to pass, that Jesus also being baptized, and praying, the heaven was opened, and the Holy Ghost descended in a bodily shape like a dove upon him, and a voice came from heaven, which said, Thou art my beloved Son; in thee I am well pleased." Following His baptism He went up into the Mount of Temptation in the wilderness where He met the devil face to face. Afterward He "came into Galilee, preaching the gospel of the kingdom of God, and saying, The time is fulfilled." Mark 1:14, 15. To what *time* was He referring? Surely it was the prophetic time of which Daniel wrote—the sixty-nine prophetic weeks, or 483 years, that were to reach to "Messiah the Prince." He had indeed come, and with His own lips He announced that the time had expired; that period foretold by the prophet, which was to mark His manifestation as the Messiah, had arrived.

Daniel foretold not only the appearance and ministry of the Messiah, but also His death. The Messiah shall be "cut off, but not for himself." Verse 26. Moffatt says, "leaving no successor." The Amplified Bible, speaking of the anointed one says, He shall be "cut off or killed, and shall have nothing [and no one belonging] to [and defending] him."

How true that was of the Messiah, the Christ! Isaiah 53:8 says, "He was cut off out of the land of the living: for the transgression of my people was he stricken." Then Gabriel tells how "the people of the prince that shall come shall destroy the city and the sanctuary." Daniel 9:26. This certainly was not Messiah the Prince, for he destroyed nothing. He gave His life to save His people from destruction. But another prince came thirty-nine years after our Lord's death who did indeed "destroy the city and the sanctuary." This was Prince Titus, son of the Roman Emperor Vespasian. Following the attack on Jerusalem by Cestius, who later retreated, Titus came to Jerusalem near the end of the Jewish war of A.D. 66 to 70. During the awful siege every detail of Jeremiah's prophecy was fulfilled, even to parents' eating of their own sons and daughters. Jeremiah 19:9.

Jesus Weeps Over Jerusalem

Knowing what awaited Jerusalem and the Jews, our Lord with a heavy heart "beheld the city, and wept over it, saying, If thou hadst known . . . the things which belong unto thy peace! but now they are hid from thine eyes. For the days shall come upon thee, that thine enemies shall cast a trench about thee, . . . and shall lay thee even with the ground, and thy children within thee; and they shall not leave in thee one stone upon another." Luke 19:41-44. "For these be the days of vengeance, that all things which are written may be fulfilled. . . . And they shall fall by the edge of the sword, and shall be led away captive into all nations: and Jerusalem shall be trodden down of the Gentiles, until the times of the Gentiles be fulfilled." Luke 21:22-24. Josephus claims that more than a million Jews perished during that terrible siege. Those not killed were sold into slavery. A monument to this brutal siege and the success of the campaign can still be seen on the Arch of Titus in Rome on which are carved representations of the spoils of the temple such as the golden candlestick and the table of shewbread. A medal was struck eulogizing the deeds of Rome in overthrowing the Jewish nation, with the legend "Judaea Capta." The Roman senate gave high praise to the victory, honoring "the divine Titus, son of the divine Vespasian the Emperor."

The Prince Who Destroyed the City

Gabriel made reference to this when he told Daniel that the prince who would come would "destroy the city and the sanctuary," by a devastating war resulting in "the overspreading of abominations." Daniel 9:26, 27. Our Lord was even more specific: "When ye therefore shall see the abomination of desolation, spoken of by Daniel the prophet, stand in the holy place, (whoso readeth, let him understand:) then let them which be in Judaea flee into the mountains." Matthew 24:15, 16. The "abomination of desolation" to which Jesus referred was the pagan symbols of the Roman army, and they did stand in the holy ground of the temple area.

Some interpreters make this part of Gabriel's prophecy apply to some antichrist of the future. However, the statement of our Lord, later confirmed by history, identifies the "abomination" as the pagan symbols of the ancient Roman army. It is regrettable that some, apparently unacquainted with the facts of history, take this portion of the prophecy and throw it far off into the future. They look for this verse to be fulfilled by one they call the great antichrist, whom they declare will appear *after* the second advent of our Lord and the "secret rapture" of the church. Such interpreters actually make a mistake similar to the one the Jews made two thousand years ago, when they failed to recognize that the prophecies concerning the Messiah were being fulfilled before their eyes. The Jews are still looking for a future Messiah, when actually the Messiah of which the Scriptures speak has already appeared in the person of our Lord Jesus Christ. He fulfilled every feature of this prophecy concerning His ministry. He was finally "cut off" when He died the cruel death of the cross in our place. Why look for some future prince to come and destroy the city of Jerusalem when everything the prophecy called for happened between A.D. 31 and 70? The details our Lord gave have met their fulfillment exactly as He said.

Abomination of Desolation Stands in the "Holy Place"

Now, note one or two important details. Jesus said that the "abomination of desolation" would "stand in the holy place." "Then let them which be in Judaea flee into the mountains." Matthew 24:15, 16. This is exactly what the faithful Christians did. They fled and saved their lives, whereas the unbelieving Jews remained in the city and most of them perished in the awful siege.

Why do some interpreters overlook the facts of history and look for some future "abomination of desolation" or antichrist after our Lord's return for His church? Why? We will seek the answer in our next chapter.

12
Messiah's Ministry and Predicted Day of His Death

Our Lord Jesus knew He would die a cruel death; but more, He knew the year, day, and hour when His death would occur. He left heaven not only to be a great teacher, but to be a great sacrifice, to die the death we deserved. Because we all have sinned, we needed someone to take the penalty of our transgression. But more, we needed One who could represent us and intercede for us at the throne of grace. The second Person of the Godhead pledged Himself to do this for us; therefore, "when the fulness of the time was come, God sent forth his Son, . . . to redeem them that were under the law, that we might receive the adoption of sons." Galatians 4:4, 5.

Christ died at the exact time specified in Daniel's prophecy. Six months before Christ began His marvelous ministry, John the Baptist came preaching and saying, "Repent ye: for the kingdom of heaven is at hand." Matthew 3:2. How did he know? He, like Jesus, was a student of the Scriptures. He knew the great time prophecies that related to both Christ and the coming antichrist, for Gabriel told Daniel about the "little horn" power that would attempt to change prophetic times and God's law—the Ten Commandments.

Prophecy Inspired the Protestant Reformation

Those same prophecies inspired the Protestant Reformers of the sixteenth century. Those reformers applied them to the papal apostasy. The books of Daniel and the Revelation were their special study, and as a writer says, they "found from our sacred books [the Scriptures] that the Pope was Antichrist, and the Church of

Rome the harlot of Babylon."—*Catholic Doctrine as Defined by the Council of Trent*, by Rev. A. Nampon, S. J., pages 103, 104.

In a tremendous endeavor to meet the challenge of these mighty preachers and teachers, two spurious interpretations were devised in order to lift the stigma from Roman Catholicism. These were known as the Preterist and Futurist interpretations. They were developed by Alcazar and Ribera. Ribera, a Jesuit theologian of the Roman Catholic Counter-Reformation, actually applied the prophecies concerning our Lord Jesus Christ to the antichrist. Speaking of the Messiah who was to be "cut off" or crucified, Gabriel said He "shall confirm the covenant with many for one week: and in the midst of the week he shall cause the sacrifice and the oblation to cease." Ribera interpreted this as the work of the antichrist who will appear in the future. But our Lord fulfilled this, first by His ministry of love, then by His sacrifice on the cross which brought an end to the sacrificial system which had foreshadowed His death.

Christ began His public ministry in A.D. 27, at the end of the sixty-nine prophetic weeks or 483 years. Gabriel said that seventy weeks, 490 years, were given specially for the Jews. "Seventy weeks of years are decreed concerning your people." Daniel 9:24, RSV. And there was still one "week" of seven years yet to be fulfilled. "In the midst" of that week, three and a half years after He began His ministry, our Lord was crucified, or "cut off out of the land of the living." Isaiah 53:8.

During those three and a half intensive years of preaching, teaching, and healing the sick He was confirming the everlasting covenant. Moreover He knew how long He had left in which to minister, for He was working to a timetable. Many times He said, "Mine hour is not yet come." But when that hour arrived, He knew it. He reminded those who came to arrest Him that He had been in the temple daily and they had not laid hands on Him. But "this is your hour," He said, "and the power of darkness." Luke 22:53.

Christ Died at the Exact Moment

Nothing that happened that night came as a surprise to the Saviour. He knew not only the day and the hour He was to die, but also the very moment of time. While hanging on the cross that Passover Day He realized that the hour of the evening sacrifice had arrived, and the sacrificial priest with knife upraised was about to take the life of the little lamb. At that moment that crucial cry came from the cross, "It is finished!" Instantly, the veil in the temple was ripped from ceiling to floor by an unseen hand. The knife dropped from the nerveless hand of the priest, and the little lamb ran away unhurt. A greater Lamb, the Lamb of God, had taken away the sin of the world! The Scripture says "in due time Christ died for the ungodly" (Weymouth, third edition, "at the right moment"). Romans 5:6.

He paid the debt of our transgressing, bearing the whole world's sin, even the awful sin of His betrayal and rejection. Some who turned against Him that day accepted Him later as their sin offering, recognizing that the One whom they crucified had paid the price of their forgiveness and by His grace had reconciled them to God.

Our Lord's ministry lasted just three and a half years, and on that Passover Day, A.D. 31, Jesus fulfilled all the elaborate services of the Hebrew ritual. His sacrifice did indeed "cause the sacrifice and the oblation to cease." Daniel 9:27. It was at the exact time— "in the midst of the week."

But there were still three and a half years remaining of that last prophetic week. During that time the disciples preached with great power in Jerusalem, and thousands responded to their message, including many of the priests. See Acts 6:7. At the end of that prophetic week, Stephen, a deacon and an eloquent preacher, was summoned to appear before the Sanhedrin because his presentation of Jesus as the Messiah was so eloquent that the people "were not able to resist the wisdom and the spirit by which he spake." Verse 10.

Stephen's Death Ends Seventy Weeks

In his defense, Stephen unfolded the history of the nation, emphasizing the salient points, bringing it right down to their own day. That powerful sermon recorded in Acts 7 is one of the high points in the New Testament story. But the elders of the Jews rushed upon him, "cast him out of the city, and stoned him." Verse 58. Stephen was the first recorded Christian martyr. The date of that tragic event was A.D. 34, just three and a half years after the crucifixion. This brought to an end of the 70 weeks "determined" or "allotted" to the Jewish people.

As we have already seen, both the 490 years and the 2,300 years began in 457 B.C. The exact fulfillment of the details given by the angel Gabriel should give every Bible student renewed confidence in the "sure word of prophecy."

Now let us pause to note again verses 26 and 27 of Daniel 9. That portion needs to be studied with particular care. It is well for us to remember that there were no punctuation marks in the original writing; all such markings having been added by translators. But for clarity let us recognize that a couple of clauses, which obviously deal with the "prince" who was to come, should be treated for what they really are—a parenthetical element: ["And the people of the prince that shall come shall destroy the city and the sanctuary; and the end thereof shall be with a flood, and unto the end of the war desolations are determined."] By placing this portion between brackets, the whole matter is clarified. For the "he" mentioned at the beginning of verse 27 properly belongs to "Messiah the Prince," not to Titus the prince of Rome who came later and destroyed the city. To misapply that part of the Scripture and apply it to some antichrist of the future really makes Christ and antichrist change places. Could we imagine a greater misfortune than this?

History Confirms the Prophecy of Seventy Weeks

Six important predictions mentioned in Daniel 9:24 were all fulfilled during the seventieth week. These six points establish without question the timing and the relationship of this great prophecy to our Lord, for not one of these occurred during the preceeding sixty-nine weeks of years. The first three had to do with the blight of sin, stating that our Lord would (1) "finish the transgression," (2) "make an end of sins [sin offerings]" through His perfect atonement, and (3) "make reconciliation for iniquity" by a substitutionary sacrifice of the Son of God. The last three deal with the glorious realities of the gospel. These are (4) "to bring in everlasting righteousness" as God's free gift of grace to all who will accept it, (5) "to seal up the vision and prophecy," and (6) "to anoint the most Holy" (Berkeley, "to consecrate the Holy of Holies"). This our Lord did following His ascension, when He entered "into heaven itself, now to appear in the presence of God for us." Hebrews 9:24.

The completion of our Lord's sacrifice and victory climaxed in the outpouring of the Holy Spirit on the Day of Pentecost. This confirmed the truth that Christ is now our great High Priest at the throne of grace. Moffatt's translation reads: "Seventy weeks of years are fixed for your people and for your sacred city, to end guilt, to complete sins, to expiate iniquity, to bring in everlasting purity, to ratify the prophetic vision, and to consecrate a most sacred Place."

While some attempt to separate the seventieth week from the sixty-ninth, looking to the future for its fulfillment in the coming of the antichrist, yet there seems no good reason for such an interpretation. Philip Mauro declares that "when a definite measure of time or space is specified by the number of units composing it, within which a certain event is to happen, . . . the units of time or space which make up the measure are to be understood as meaning continuously and successively." This he declares to be "an absolute rule."—*The Seventy Weeks and the Great Tribulation.*

While commonsense and sound exegesis emphasize the wisdom of this, history also proves the accuracy of such interpretation.

In Exodus 30:26-30 and 40:9-13 we have the account of the anointing and consecration of the Mosaic tabernacle before the services began. And in Hebrews 8:1, 2; 9:11, 15 we have the record of the heavenly sanctuary where Christ ministers, which was consecrated at the beginning of His priestly work there.

Christ's Ministry of Reconciliation and Judgment

Just as in the type there were two phases of ministry, reconciliation and judgment, so our heavenly High Priest has a ministry which begins with reconciliation and will climax in the work of judgment. The two apartments in the earthly sanctuary, the "holy place" and the "most holy place," represent these two vital phases of our Lord's ministry. While the earthly sanctuary was small in its construction, it typified great realities in His sacrifice and priestly ministry. When Gabriel said, "Unto two thousand and three hundred days; then shall the sanctuary be cleansed," he had reference not to a Day of Atonement (Yom Kippur) of the earthly sanctuary, but to the Day of Atonement of the heavenly sanctuary.

Just as there came a day in ancient Israel when the high priest performed the ceremonial service of cleansing, so in the heavenly sanctuary there is also a cleansing, and this will be by "better sacrifices" than those offered in the earthly sanctuary. Hebrews 9:23. The Scripture says plainly that "without shedding of blood is no remission" or forgiveness. Verse 22. The earthly sanctuary was cleansed by the blood of animals, but "heavenly things themselves with better sacrifices than these." Verse 23. In ancient Israel the day of cleansing, the Day of Atonement, was a very solemn occasion. If anyone on that day refused to confess his sins, he was "cut off" from the congregation. It was therefore a day of judgment and is so regarded by orthodox Jews even to this day. Gabriel could just as easily have said "unto two thousand three hundred years; then shall judgment day begin," for that is what the statement implies.

Termination of the Prophecy of 2,300 Days

We have already noted the marvelous accuracy of the shorter prophecy of seventy prophetic weeks or 490 years which ended in A.D. 34. Subtracting 490 years from the longer period of 2,300 years leaves 1,810 years. Finding the termination of the longer period is very easy. Just add 1810 to 34 and we come to the year 1844, when the sanctuary would be "cleansed." At that time our great High Priest, "Messiah the Prince," entered upon his closing work as our Mediator.

The "everlasting gospel" going to all the world today is, "Fear God, and give glory to him; for the hour of his judgment is come." Revelation 14:7. The apostle Paul preached about a judgment to come, declaring that God "hath appointed a day, in the which he will judge the world in righteousness by that man whom he hath ordained; whereof he hath given assurance unto all men, in that he raised him from the dead." Acts 17:31. Messiah, the Prince who was raised from the dead, is the appointed One to judge the world.

How Shall We Stand in the Judgment?

When the Ancient of Days took His place to preside over that august assembly, "the judgment was set, and the books were opened." Daniel 7:10. In those books is a record of every life lived on earth; and in the closing work of our Lord in the heavenly sanctuary these records are examined, decisions reached, and reward apportioned. When our Lord appears in glory, He comes bringing His rewards with Him. Revelation 22:11, 12. These words of Scripture in Ecclesiastes 12:13, 14 are relevant and sobering! "Let us hear the conclusion of the whole matter: Fear God, and keep his commandments. . . . For God shall bring every work into judgment, with every secret thing, whether it be good, or whether it be evil."

When we think of the Judge of all the earth reviewing the cases in that judgment, it is reassuring to recall the words of Jesus: "He that heareth my word, and believeth on him that sent me, hath everlasting life, and shall not come into condemnation." John 5:24. If we are living the life of overcomers, then we can claim our Lord's promise that we shall be "clothed in white raiment." His assurance is, "I will not blot out *his* name out of the book of life, but I will confess *his* name before my Father." Revelation 3:5.

Sad to say, some will have their names blotted out of the book of life because they are not living the life of victory through God's grace. As we noticed earlier, the great Judge opens before the intelligent universe all the records of His dealings with men and angels. Thus He vindicates His own character, "that every mouth may be stopped." No word can ever be justly spoken against the justice and the mercy of our great God and Saviour.

Sensing what is going on now in the heavenly sanctuary, every one of us should examine our lives, making sure that we are living victoriously by the power of the indwelling Spirit of God.

13
Divine Intervention in International Politics

We have now reached the closing section of the book of Daniel. The last three chapters belong together. Chapter 10 is an introduction to the largest, most involved prophecy in the whole Bible, reaching from Daniel's day to the end of time.

The revelation came to him in the third year of the reign of King Cyrus, 535 B.C. The prophet is specific in his description of what happened. He uses his own Hebrew name, Daniel, as well as Belteshazzar, the name given him by Nebuchadnezzar. The Babylonian Empire had passed; and, although Daniel was about 90 years of age, he was still an officer of state, but now in the empire of Persia. He had already received visions vital to his nation, but what was now revealed was tremendously important. He had been "mourning three full weeks."

During that long fast he had taken "no pleasant bread" and had abstained from the normal comforts of life. He was greatly burdened for his nation. Cyrus had issued a decree permitting the Jews to return and begin rebuilding the temple in Jerusalem. The builders had met with such stern opposition from their neighbors, the Samaritans, however, that the work, which had begun with such enthusiasm, had temporarily stopped. This weighed heavily on Daniel's heart, and he gave himself to prayer and fasting. He had chosen some place of retirement on the bank of the river Hiddekel or Tigris, probably close to where it joins the Euphrates, about 100 miles north of the Persian Gulf. It being the Passover season, followed by the Feast of Unleavened Bread, he was vividly reminded of Israel's deliverance from Egyptian bondage nearly a thousand years earlier. He was certain that the same God who so miraculously worked for His people in the past was able to meet the opposition of present enemies. Thus the prophet prayed.

Daniel Beholds Deity

Looking up, he saw a mighty celestial Being in dazzling brightness wearing a golden girdle. His eyes appeared like flaming torches and His limbs like burnished brass. The sight was overwhelming. He spoke with a voice as of a multitude. Here was One who surpassed in splendor even the angel Gabriel.

Comparing the words of Daniel 10:5, 6 with Ezekiel 1:24-28 and Revelation 1:13-16, we cannot doubt that Daniel, Ezekiel, and John were each describing the same One. The Lord of all the earth had come in person to His praying servant on the bank of the river. Little wonder the prophet was overcome with fear.

Daniel tells us that he was alone when he received this vision of majestic splendor. As he swooned and fell to his knees, he heard a reassuring voice saying, "O Daniel, a man greatly beloved, understand the words that I speak unto thee, and stand upright."

This was not the voice of the celestial Being he had just seen in vision, but the familiar voice of Gabriel who had appeared to him on other occasions. The angel continued: "Fear not, Daniel: for from the first day that thou didst set thine heart to understand, . . . thy words were heard, and I am come for thy words" (Berkeley, "I have come in response to your prayers"). How wonderful to know that when we seek God in earnest prayer as did Daniel, heavenly angels bring the answer.

Three weeks had passed since the prophet began his prayer vigil. Why the long delay? We now enter one of the most profound revelations in all the Bible. In verse 13 we catch a brief glimpse of the unseen struggle between God's loyal angels and Satan's rebel hosts. The Scriptures picture these forces as real and substantial. The apostle Paul said: "For our fight is not against any physical enemy: it is against organizations and powers that are spiritual. We are up against the unseen power that controls this dark world, and spiritual agents from the very headquarters of evil." Ephesians 6:12, Phillips. The same apostle reveals that behind the idols of the heathen are demons to whom they make their sacrifices. 1 Corinthians 10:20.

Demon Powers Seek to Thwart God's Plans

So real are these demonic powers that they delayed even the mighty Gabriel from changing the circumstances to make possible the favorable answer to Daniel's prayer. Notice the angel's words: "The prince of the kingdom of Persia withstood me." The word "prince," *sar* in Hebrew, occurs over 400 times in the Old Testament. It means "ruler, governor, or military commander." The prince of whom Gabriel speaks could well have been Cyrus. But influencing him was another unseen power, "the prince of the power of the air," the one who seeks to control this dark world of sin, the author of evil—Satan himself. The meaning of the word Satan is *adversary*.

Gabriel disclosed now to Daniel that not until Michael came to his aid was he able to move upon the heart of King Cyrus to deal with the enemies of the Jews and permit the rebuilding program to proceed. Who is this Michael, "one of the chief princes," (or "the first of the princes")? The name appears three times in the book of Daniel. The earliest occurrence in the Bible story is when "Michael the archangel" contended with the devil about the body of Moses. Jude 9. In that contention Michael said to the devil, "The Lord rebuke thee." "Michael" means "Who [is] like God?"

It is the Archangel who calls the dead to life at the second advent. Jesus declared that all who are in their graves shall hear His voice and come forth. John 5:29. In Daniel 12 Michael is called "the great prince which standeth for the children of thy people." Putting these scriptures together, we must agree with Melanchthon the great Reformer, who "insisted" that Michael should be identified with Christ Himself. Certainly Christ is the One who has stood for Daniel's people through all their struggles. As Redeemer, Deliverer, Sustainer, and coming King, He will at last lead His people through the pearly gates into the Holy City.

Who Is Michael?

Gabriel told Daniel, "There is none that holdeth with me in these things, but Michael your prince." Daniel 10:21. This has led some to believe that Michael is in a special sense "the guardian angel of the Jews." But He is the One who calls not only Jews back to life, but all who have died in the hope of the resurrection. Michael, "the great prince," is also called the "Prince of life," (Acts 3:15), the "Prince of princes" (Daniel 8:25), "Messiah the Prince" (Daniel 9:25), the "Prince of Peace " (Isaiah 9:6), and the "prince of the kings of the earth" (Revelation 1:5). He is greater than Gabriel, for He created the angels and every other creature in the universe. Significantly, the only time He is called Michael is when He is matching His power against the prince of evil, and each time He emerges the mighty Conqueror.

In warfare it is vital to know the strategy of the enemy. So in our warfare against Satan and his hosts we need to know something of the strategy of these forces of evil. We need even more than knowledge; we need "the whole armour of God." Ephesians 6:11. Speaking of his victory, the angel told Daniel that he remained at the Persian court and, according to the Knox translation, "was left master of the field."

"I am come to make thee understand what shall befall thy people in the latter days: for yet the vision is for many days," said Gabriel. Daniel 10:14. Moffatt translates it: "Now I am here to let you know what is to befall your people at the end of the ages; for this vision relates to the far future."

Daniel's people were, of course, the Jews. According to the angel something special would happen to these people in the "latter days," that is, "at the end of the ages." The long prophecy of chapter 11 traces the events which lead to the final crisis for the Jews and the whole world. Many nations are introduced in this prophecy, not because of their importance nationally, but simply because of their relationship to Israel through the centuries, either as persecutors or deliverers. This will continue through all time, and at "the end of the ages," "the latter days," "thy people shall be delivered, every one that shall be found written in the book." Daniel 12:1. In that great day, race will mean nothing. To "be found written in the book" will mean everything.

Daniel—Prophet "Greatly Beloved"

The presence and appearance of the celestial Being had left the prophet speechless and in a state of prostration. After Gabriel had tried to encourage Daniel, and had disclosed to him what was happening behind the scenes, the prophet was overwhelmed still by the revelation. He needed not only to be encouraged, but supernaturally strengthened—this time by a being described as one who appeared as a man, saying: "O man greatly beloved, fear not: . . . be strong." Now Daniel was ready for the full revelation of that which "is noted in the scripture of truth." Verses 19, 21.

Prophets had written, and other prophets were still to write, concerning the long ages of suffering and oppression, not only for Israel but for all God's people. But in "the end of the days," or at "the crisis at the close," (Daniel 12:9, Moffatt) in all God's children His character will be vindicated, His purpose fully understood, and His people delivered eternally.

This is the theme of all revelation, but especially of this vision of the eleventh chapter, this most interesting prophecy which the angel was about to unfold. Before he did, he asked Daniel, "Do you know why I have come unto you?" Daniel 10:20, RSV. It was not only to give the prophet a wonderful revelation, but also "to fight with the prince of Persia." Read these words with particular care. The Hebrew word *im*, "with," in the Septuagint is "*meta*," meaning not "against," but "in common with," "alongside." For three weeks the king of Persia had been influenced by demonic powers. It was not until Michael, the preexistent Son of God, came to his aid that Gabriel was able to visit Daniel. Now, Gabriel said that as soon as he had delivered his full message he would return to the king, thus helping to carry out God's purpose in the rebuilding of Jerusalem.

Gabriel also foretold, "when I am gone forth," (i.e., when he would withdraw his support from Persia,) "lo, the prince [or ruler] of Grecia shall come." So long as it was in the plan of God, Persia would stand. But at last Greece would become a world kingdom, the detailed history of which the angel was about to reveal.

We will study this in the next chapter.

14
Political Intrigue
Divides Greek Empire

The last two chapters of Daniel are a fascinating forecast of history. So plain is this prophecy that Porphyry, Syrian sophist of the third century A.D., claimed it could not possibly have been written before the events occurred, but that it must be the work of some "pious Jew" pretending to be a prophet. "No man could forecast history with such exactitude," he said. Following his lead, the critics of our day make the same claim.

While Daniel 11 is both remarkably intricate and precise, it is not beyond our understanding. The prophecies presented in earlier chapters are now more fully developed as Gabriel unfolds the details of this, the most complex prophecy in God's Word. When the Babylonian Empire collapsed, Cyrus, the Persian conqueror, apparently had appointed Darius the Mede, probably his uncle and father-in-law, as king of Babylon, where he reigned for two years until his death. The angel Gabriel, who had been working so definitely in influencing King Cyrus to suppress the enemies of the Jewish rebuilding program in Jerusalem, now tells Daniel he had also stood by Darius the Mede to strengthen him. Verse 1.

The essence of the prophecy begins with these words: "Three more kings will appear in Persia, and the fourth will far surpass all the others in wealth; and when he has extended his power through his wealth, he will rouse the whole world against the kingdom of Greece." Daniel 11:2, NEB.

The Medo-Persian Empire was well established with Cyrus as the ruling king when Daniel received this vision. The four kings therefore are Cambyses, son of Cyrus, who ruled from 530-522 B.C.;

Smerdis, the impostor, who ruled only seven months; Darius Hystaspes, i.e. Darius the Great, 522-486 B.C.; and Xerxes, Ahasuerus of Esther 1:1, 486-465 B.C.

Xerxes was both wealthy and self-assured. Having amassed an army, which Herodotus says consisted of more than 5,000,000 men [a modern estimate says 250,000 men], he declared war on Greece, but suffered a humiliating defeat at Salamis in 480 B.C. Persia never really recovered from it. After Xerxes came nine minor kings, but the prophecy takes no account of them.

Alexander Builds a New Empire

The next outstanding ruler, destined to "do according to his will," was Alexander the Great; who in eight years welded the Greek city-states into an empire.

The angel described him as a "mighty king" who would "do according to his will." Verse 3. "But as soon as he is established," the angel said, "his kingdom will be shattered and split up north, south, east and west. It will not pass to his descendants, nor will any of his successors have an empire like his." Verse 4, NEB.

Alexander advanced as far as the plains of northern India. But his soldiers, having been away from home for years, begged him to return. He did, expecting to set up his world headquarters in Babylon. But in the midst of his conquests he contracted a severe fever following a drunken spree. He could conquer the world but not himself, and he died in 323 B.C. His ambitious projects collapsed and went into eclipse, as we have seen. The empire was rent by civil strife for the next twenty years. The words of the prophecy are exact: the kingdom would be divided, but "not to his posterity."

Alexander's four leading generals, after long and complicated struggles, divided the empire "toward the four winds of heaven" in 301 B.C. Lysimachus took the north; Ptolemy the south; Seleucus the east; and Cassander the west. These were later reduced to three; Seleucus having swallowed up that of Lysimachus. That enlarged kingdom then became, in the language of the prophecy, the "king of the north," with Egypt and its environs the "king of the south." Throughout the centuries, in spite of wars and revolutions which brought changes in boundaries and rulers, the prophecy refers to them as "the king of the north" and "the king of the south."

Historians call the continual conflicts of these times the Syrian Wars, Judea being a buffer state between the two.

A Patched-up Peace

At last the king of the north and that of the south made peace when Ptolemy II, called Philadelphus, gave his daughter Berenice in marriage to Antiochus Theos, grandson of Seleucus. "They shall join themselves together," says the prophecy; "for the king's daughter of the south shall come to the king of the north to make an agreement." To seal the agreement, Laodice, wife of Antiochus, was divorced and her children declared illigitimate—a poor foundation for a lasting peace. A large dowry accompanied Berenice. Later, when her father died, Antiochus divorced her and took back his former wife Laodice. Fearing further disgrace this reclaimed wife had her husband poisoned and her own son placed on the throne. Not long afterward she had her rival Berenice assassinated together with the Egyptian friends who had come with her.

The remarkable accuracy of the prophecy is evident: "She shall be given up, and they that brought her, and he that begat her" ("her child," NEB) Verse 6. "Then another shoot from the same stock as hers will appear in his father's place," says the prophecy. Verse 7, NEB.

Ptolemy Euergetes, who came to the Egyptian throne upon the death of his father Philadelphus, determined to avenge the death of his sister Berenice. With a large army he invaded the north and marched eastward as far as Babylon. He was compelled to return to Egypt because of an insurrection, but he brought with him from the kingdom of Seleucus a large booty, including 2,000 gold and silver images and 4,000 talents of gold, 40,000 talents of silver, and precious vessels which Cambyses of Persia had carried into Syria 280 years earlier. It was then that the people named him "Euergetes," meaning "benefactor." These ruling and warring families were not Syrians or Egyptians; they were Greeks, descendants of Alexander's generals.

During all these wars Daniel's people, the Jews, knew little peace. But despite the warfare and intrigue surrounding them they remained in the Holy Land. Moreover they were able to check constantly the accuracy of Daniel's prophecies. More important still, during these decades of intrigue, they gave to the world the famous translation of the Old Testament, the Septuagint (LXX). The Hebrew religion and literature was thus made available to the nations around them.

After Ptolemy's crushing defeat of the Syrians the area enjoyed a few years respite from war. But Seleucus Callinicus, having reestablished his power in Asia, made a foolhardy expedition into Egypt in 242 B.C. His forces were routed, and he lost his fleet in a severe storm. He was then obliged to return to his own land, thus fulfilling in detail the prophecy of verse 9.

Not long afterward, Callinicus, Seleucus II, fell from his horse and died. He was succeeded by his son Ceraunus, Seleucus III, who reigned only three years; then his brother Antiochus III came to the throne. These brothers shared their father's determination to repair the national fortunes and avenge their humiliating defeat.

Antiochus commenced with such a show of strength that he was called Antiochus Magnus, "the Great." His reign was marked by incessant warfare. He took advantage of the weak and indecisive king of Egypt, Ptolemy IV, Philopater. Having raised a great force, he launched an offensive against the king of the south. The Syrians seemed irresistible, and as the prophecy declares, he did "overflow and pass through" Gaza, Phoenicia, and Judea. With perhaps as much as 70,000 infantry and 5,000 cavalry, Antiochus advanced to the Egyptian border. At the frontiers of Raphia, in 217 B.C., his forces were surprisingly defeated and his army was routed, leaving 10,000 slain and 4,000 taken prisoner.

King of the South Profanes Jewish Temple

Ptolemy, elated over his success, continued to fulfill prophecy by annexing Palestine. The Jews were thus forced again to change their allegiance from Syria to Egypt. Instead of moving on to consolidate his gains, the Egyptian ruler, the king of the south, made peace with Antiochus, king of the north. He insulted the Jews by entering the temple area and attempting to offer sacrifice, a rite reserved for consecrated priests only. When he insisted on entering the holy of holies he "fell speechless to the ground," according to legend, and was carried out half dead. Disgraced and furious, he returned to Alexandria. In this city, a stronghold for the Jews, he instituted a murderous persecution against these unfortunate people, demanding that they worship his idols. More than 40,000 Jews preferred death to idolatry. The prophecy said he would "cast down tens of thousands."

Such slaughter God could not let go unpunished. So "after certain years," the king of the north, Antiochus, after strengthening himself, brought many elephants from India and again invaded Egypt. This time his attack was indeed "greater than the former." Many others joined the forces of the Syrian king, including some violent Jews who called themselves "the Sons of Tobias." These refractory Jews seemed to think they might establish this vision of Daniel and would ultimately regain their independence as a nation. They found their hopes frustrated, however, and their plans overthrown. Many perished in the ensuing conflicts. Antiochus, using Judea as a station from which to menace Egypt, left his armies there, and the little land of Judea, the scene of bitter hostilities between north and south, was laid waste.

"And in those times there shall many stand up against the king of the south" says the prophecy. With the death of both the king and the queen of Egypt, probably by poisoning, and a four-year-old son being placed on the throne, Antiochus, the master tactician, saw the possibility of revenge for his overthrow at Raphia.

To make sure of victory he made an alliance with Philip V of Macedonia, and together these kings gathered a greater army than before, intending to divide the territory between them. But they failed to recognize that the child king of Egypt was under the legal guardianship of the Roman Senate, which promptly declared war on Philip V and forced Antiochus to make peace with Egypt, king of the south.

Verse 15 speaks of "the most fenced cities" (NEB, "a fortified town"). This city was Gaza, which bravely stood out against Antiochus. But at last it, too, was forced to surrender as the prophecy had declared: "the arms of the south shall not withstand." Moreover, Hannibal, the veteran enemy of Rome, joined his forces with Antiochus. Next we find Rome declaring war against Syria in 191 B.C. Defeated by this rising world power, Antiochus was forced to accept the terms the Romans offered him, which included the payment of a large yearly tribute to the Senate. In addition, his young son, later known as the notorious Antiochus Epiphanes, had to go to Rome as a hostage. Thus Rome, the fourth world empire, comes into the prophetic picture. From now on to the end of time this power will have a prominent place both in prophecy and history.

The Rising Power of Rome

The Scripture introduces this new power under the description: "He that cometh against him shall do according to his own will." Verse 16. This expression was also used in reference to Alexander the Great. Verse 3. But the context shows that here it alludes neither to him nor to Antiochus Epiphanes, as some commentators suggest, though it would be hard to find a more accurate description of Rome than in the last part of the verse: "And none shall stand before him: and he shall stand in the glorious land, which by his hand shall be consumed."

Although the king of the north had conquered the Egyptian forces, neither he nor any other kingdom could stand before the growing power of Rome. Syria eventually became a Roman province under Pompey in 65 B.C. Judea came under the full jurisdiction of Rome in 63 B.C. Nearly a century earlier, in 161., the Jews had entered into an alliance, called the League. By this they hoped to protect themselves against the Syrian persecutions under Antiochus Epiphanes, son of Antiochus the Great, who, as mentioned above, had been a hostage in Rome. His rule was marked by cruelties and indignities.

That alliance with Rome proved in the end to be the Jews' undoing. This is the case when the people of God line up with the world. Had the Jewish leaders heeded the counsel of Isaiah and Jeremiah, history would have been written differently.

Every sentence in verses 17 to 22 adds to the prophetic picture. It is an accurate forecast of the great events in Rome's march to world empire. It is strange that certain interpreters fail to see the great events in the history of Rome, so accurately predicted in this prophecy. Instead they go in search of incidents in the life and work of Antiochus Epiphanes. An example of this is found in the voluminous notes in this chapter in the RSV Annotated Bible. If one did not know better, he would be led by such commentators to regard this weak and at times half-witted king, who reigned only a few years, as the central figure in this long and wonderful prophecy. It would be strange if we did not know that this whole system of interpretation is a design on the part of the great enemy of truth and righteousness to lead men's minds from a true understanding of history in order to lift the stigma from the antichrist of the centuries.

Thomas Newton's rendering of verse 17 is "He," that is Rome, "shall set his face to enter by force the whole kingdom."—*Dissertations on the Prophecies*, Vol. 1, p. 356. All that was left of the "whole kingdom" of Alexander was Egypt, Thrace, Macedonia, and Judea. Syria had already been conquered by the Romans, who then set out to force Egypt, the king of the south, into subjection. Our next chapter will trace briefly Rome's rulership in the light of this prophecy.

15
Prophecy's Forecast of Rome's Rulership

When Ptolemy Auletes died in 51 B.C. he left the throne to his daughter Cleopatra and her brother Ptolemy XII, a lad of ten years. The king's will provided that they should marry each other—then a common practice in Egyptian royalty—and reign jointly. Because they were young, the guardianship of Rome was sought. The people appointed Pompey as overseer of the court. Three years later trouble broke out between Pompey and Julius Caesar, which ended in the Battle of Pharsalus. Pompey was defeated and fled to Egypt. Caesar followed him there. Pompey was killed, and Caesar found Egypt in commotion. Ptolemy and Cleopatra were quarreling. She claimed that he had deprived her of her share in the government. Caesar gave orders that the armies of each had to disband and that both Ptolemy and Cleopatra appear before him and then abide by his decision. Advocates were appointed for each side to plead for their respective parties. Cleopatra determined to conquer Caesar by feminine wiles rather than by military force or advocate's arguments. She had the right to be heard if Caesar was to be the judge. So she arranged for a boatman to take her to him.

To reach his presence undetected, she had Apollodonus, her Sicilian slave, wrap her up in a cloth and tie the package with thongs. Then raising it to his "Herculean shoulders" he sought Caesar's apartments, claiming to have a special present for the Roman general. Being admitted into Caesar's presence, he laid the burden at his feet and made a speedy exit. When this animated bundle was unbound there stood the beautiful and voluptuous Cleopatra before him.

The prophecy of chapter eleven could well refer to this, where we read in verse 17: "And he shall give him the daughter of women, corrupting her" (margin, "to corrupt"). While Caesar was past fifty and Cleopatra merely twenty-two, she was as ambitious as he. She became his mistress and bore him a son. His infatuation for the queen kept him much longer in Egypt than his affairs asked for. This may have been a contributing factor in the plot to assassinate him at the zenith of his power. The next verse seems to express this thought: "A prince shall cause the reproach offered by him to cease; moreover, he shall cause his reproach to turn upon him." Verse 18, RV. And is that not what happened? As he passed into the Senate chamber, Cassius and Brutus, outwardly friends of Caesar, signaled to the conspirators, and almost instantly twenty daggers were buried in his body, leaving the greatest general in Rome's history silent in death in the Forum.

Caesar Returns to Italy

Before that murder, however, many other details in the prophecy were to be fulfilled. Verse 18 says: "Shall he turn his face unto the isles, and shall take many." Some see in the expression "the isles" nothing more than the coastlands of northern Africa, but Caesar had conquered more than Egypt; his aim was to rule the world. When trouble broke out in the Cimmerian Bosporus, Julius Caesar was called into action. Later he landed in Sicily with legions of men and 6,000 horses. He then set sail for Africa, appearing at the Republicans' camp, and summoned them to surrender to "Caesar the Imperator." They refused, saying they acknowledged no imperator but Scipio. War ensued, which Caesar won. He then claimed the north coast of Africa.

One of the tragic losses of Caesar's wars was the destruction of the famous Alexandrian library of nearly 400,000 volumes, a tremendous collection for those days. It happened this way. Pothimus, chief minister of state for Egypt, was afraid of Caesar's influence. Fearing that Julius might give Cleopatra complete power, he instigated a sedition which resulted in an attempt to burn the Roman fleet. Caesar retorted by burning theirs. Some of the burning vessels were driven by the wind near the quay, and the fire spread to some of the city's buildings, including the grand library.

The prophecy also mentions that the "upright ones" would be with him. Antipater of Idumea joined Caesar against Egypt, bringing with him 3,000 Jews. The Jews held the frontier gateways into the country through which the Roman armies were permitted to pass without interruption. All of this had a bearing on the outcome. Commenting on this, Uriah Smith says: "A decisive battle was fought near the Nile by the fleets of Egypt and Rome, resulting in complete victory for Caesar. Ptolemy, attempting to escape, was drowned in the river. Alexandria and all Egypt then submitted to the victor. Rome had now entered into and absorbed the entire original kingdom of Alexander."—*Daniel and the Revelation*, 1944 ed., page 251.

Julius Caesar Assassinated

Having accomplished so much for the empire, Julius Caesar, as the prophecy said, turned "his face toward the fort of his own land." Verse 19. Upon arriving in Rome he was made dictator for life. Having been granted many other honors, he was in fact absolute sovereign of the empire. But the same Scripture says, "he shall stumble and fall, and not be found." How true that was! This man who had fought and won fifty battles, taken more than 1,000 cities at the cost of 1,192,000 of his soldiers, fell not amid the strife of the battlefield, but just when he thought all was well.

The night before his assassination in 44 B.C. he was dining with Lepidus and a group of friends. In casual conversation Caesar was asked, "What is the best way to die?" "Suddenly," he replied as he continued to sign letters. The next day, at noon, the mighty Caesar, the man who had done "according to his own will," lay dead at the foot of Pompey's statue in the Roman Forum.

As Julius Caesar had no legitimate sons, Octavius, his nephew whom he had adopted, became his heir and succeeded him. Announcing publicly his adoption by his uncle, he immediately took his name, which from that time became the title for the Roman emperors. He joined Mark Antony and Lepidus to avenge the death of Caesar. The three formed the *triumvirate* form of government. When the other two members died, Octavius became emperor. The Senate also conferred on him the title "Augustus."

For some years the so-called Republic of Rome was torn with

internal strife and war, but at length discipline and peace were established. The Battle of Actium in 31 B.C., left Augustus sole ruler. He proved both wise and strong. He replaced chaos and anarchy by imperial organization which lasted with varying vicissitudes for the next four centuries. He possessed the unusual ability to levy taxes without upsetting the populace too much. His taxes were light but universal, and they supplied the funds for the imperial government. He was both clever and efficient. As an empire-wide enroller for taxation he comes prominently into the Bible story. Note the exact description in Daniel 11:20: "Then shall stand up in his estate [Julius Caesar's place] a raiser of taxes in the glory of the kingdom."

Caesar Augustus Enrolls the World

The special importance of this prophecy is manifested by its remarkable place in the history of salvation. "It came to pass in those days, that there went out a decree from Caesar Augustus, that all the world should be taxed." Luke 2:1. It was that decree which brought Joseph and Mary to Bethlehem. While they were there, Jesus was born. "All the world" is a sweeping statement, and the one who enforced it should surely, above all others, have the title "a raiser of taxes." Again we pause to comment on the strange lengths some commentators go seeking for other incidents and personalities to fit the prophecy differently, simply to avoid applying these verses to Rome. Thus unwittingly perhaps, they corrupt the truth and lose the real message which Gabriel gave to Daniel especially for the last days. They attempt to make Heliodorus the Syrian treasurer this "raiser of taxes," because he hated the Jews and inflicted very heavy taxes on them. However, this happened more than a century earlier than the context justifies. It also ignores the fact that Luke 2:1 seems to be a direct allusion to Daniel's prophecy. Besides, the taxing of Heliodorus was limited to the Jews, whereas that of Augustus extended to "all the world," including Palestine. Moreover, this "raiser of taxes" appeared "in the glory of the kingdom."

Rome reached the pinnacle of her greatness during the Augustan Age. It was a time of peace and comparative justice. Unlimited luxury was reined, and law and order were established. The temple of Janus at Rome was shut for the first time since 235 B.C. This signified that all the world was at peace. How does this compare to the rather insignificant kingdom of Syria, with its even less illustrious Heliodorus, which some commentators see as the fulfillment of this great prophecy?

Augustus died, as the prophecy foretold, "neither in anger, nor in battle." Julius Caesar met his death in anger, but Augustus died peacefully in bed at the high age of 76, his wife being by his side.

He had gone to the quiet resort town of Nola for health reasons and while there suffered a heart attack. His wife, Livia, did not notify the Senate, as she was eager for her son to become emperor. She knew the well-deserved contempt in which he was held by so many but was determined to prevent any attempt to place someone else on the throne.

Tiberius was a contrast in every way with Augustus. The prophecy says plainly: "In his estate shall stand up a vile person, to whom they shall not give the honour of the kingdom: but he shall come in peaceably, and obtain the kingdom by flatteries." Verse 21.

He was indeed a "vile person" (RSV, "contemptible person"). Seneca declared that Tiberius was intoxicated only once in his life, and that was all the time! He showed few qualities of a ruler. When Livia urged Augustus to nominate Tiberius, her son by a former marriage, to succeed him as emperor, he replied, "Your son is too vile to wear the purple of Rome." Agrippa, a highly respected man, was nominated instead, but he died before the death of Augustus.

Livia, not to be outdone, gained her end "by flatteries" as the prophecy declared. She organized a royal party in honor of the emperor. When things were at their height, and after a flattering speech about her husband's fine qualities, she repeated her request for Tiberius's nomination for the throne. Augustus, unwilling to hurt her feelings, made the official announcement. His sudden demise left no time to change anything. So Tiberius, the "vile person," came to the throne. To him however they did "not give the honour of the kingdom," for he lost the respect of the citizens of Rome.

Christ Crucified During Reign of Tiberius

The next verse tells of "overwhelming forces" (Berkeley) being swept away. The reign of Tiberius was marked by frequent revolutions and violence. "Armies shall be utterly swept away before him and broken, and the prince of the covenant also." Verse 22, RSV. This is "Messiah the Prince," who was to "confirm the covenant with many for one week." Daniel 9:25-27. During the reign of Tiberius our Lord was crucified. Pilate owed his governorship of Judea only to the favor of Tiberius, the uncle of his wife. So, when someone in the crowd called out, "If thou let this man go, thou art not Caesar's friend" (John 19:12), he gave in to the demands of the Jewish leaders. This settled the verdict. Pilate, the vacillating princeling who knew that Jesus was innocent, gave the order for Him to be scourged and crucified.

Christ, the Prince of the covenant, began His ministry in the autumn of A.D. 27, which terminated three-and-a-half years later in the spring of A.D. 31. The power responsible for our Lord's crucifixion was the one that 192 years before had entered into the league, the alliance with Judah, in 161 B.C. At that time the Romans were a "small people" as the prophecy says, but they began to "work deceitfully," as verse 23 foretold.

Having traced the story of Rome from verses 14-22 until the most important, the substitutionary death of the Messiah, "the prince of the covenant," the angel, in order to impress the significance of that event, now reaches back to another milestone for the Jewish people, the entering into the league, i.e., the alliance of friendship and mutual assistance between Judea and Rome. Josephus tells how the Jews, led by the high priest, entered into this league with enthusiasm—*Antiquities*, XII: Chap. 10.

The prophecy predicted that he shall enter peaceably even upon the fattest places of the province; and he shall do that which his fathers have not done." Posing as defenders of the weak, the Romans were the first in a large way to capitalize on the hopes of oppressed peoples. They soon became "the world's national referee," as one writer expressed it. By offering a sense of security they extended their authority from Northern Africa to England, and from Spain to Palestine. Whole countries were bequeathed to the Roman Senate. *Pax Romana* extended to the civilized world.

The last part of verse 24 says, "even for a time." If we regard this "time" as prophetic it would be 360 years, according to Biblical reckoning as noted in earlier chapters. Counting from September 2,

31 B.C., when the decisive Battle of Actium was fought, from which Augustus dated his reign, a prophetic "time" of 360 years, would bring us to A.D. 330. In this year Constantine removed the capital from Rome to Constantinople, an event regarded by many as a fulfillment of verse 24.

During most of those 360 years the empire was marked by intrigue. Before Octavian, Caesar Augustus, came to power, there was keen rivalry between him and his brother-in-law Mark Antony, who also had come under the spell of Cleopatra. These two rivals are described in verses 26 and 27. While formerly in alliance, Antony and Octavius each aspired to complete dominion. While they could outwardly enjoy "sitting at the same table, they will lie to each other with advantage to neither." Verse 27, NEB. Octavia, sister of Octavius, declared she had married Antony in the hope of keeping these two men as friends. True to the prophecy, however, it did not "prosper." In a very short time Antony and Cleopatra, for whom he had divorced his wife, were both dead, he by a self-inflicted dagger and she by the bite of an asp (probably an Egyptian cobra) smuggled into her presence in a basket of fruit.

One of the last campaigns of Octavius, by the authority of the Senate, was his war against Cleopatra, which also meant war with Antony. The latter, sensing the impending crisis, set sail for Athens, issuing orders everywhere for men and ships. Antony's fleet was anchored in the Ambracian Gulf, while his land forces encamped on the north shore of the inlet, a most unhealthful spot—one which caused the death of many troops. Some of his chief officers were won over to Octavian. The rest, disgusted by Cleopatra's influence on Antony, deserted him.

Antony, urged by Cleopatra, made his attack from the sea. Soon the wind fell, however, and his large, nearly unmanageable vessels proved no match for Octavian's light oar-propelled ships. When at last the wind sprang up, the Egyptian queen with sixty ships set sail for the south. Antony, realizing that the situation was hopeless, sprang from his ship onto a light galley and followed. By nightfall the remnants of the Egyptian fleet were destroyed by fire. Rome had conquered, and Octavian was the hero.

If we are right in applying these verses to Rome, then we should note with care two uses of the word "return." The first related to

Octavian. Returning after his conquest of Egypt, he came back "with great riches," so valuable it is claimed, that the value of money dropped 50 percent while the price of products increased 100 percent.

Yet there was another, more significant "return" when Titus returned covered with glory, having overthrown Judah and scattered the Jews everywhere. It certainly is true that his heart was "against the holy covenant."

Jerusalem Destroyed by Rome

The destruction of Jerusalem under orders from Vespasian was the next great enterprise of Rome. Daniel's people, the Jews, had been given unusual liberty by Augustus. This was lost under Vespasian and his son Titus, however. Moffatt describes this power as "doing as he pleases with the sacred nation," which Rome certainly did. The Jewish war broke out in A.D. 66, and when it concluded four years later the magnificent temple was no more. Many items of sacred furniture were taken to Rome as trophies of war.

The siege of Jerusalem by Titus was a tragic fulfillment of the prophecy of Moses in Deuteronomy 28:52-55. The Roman general swore "the extermination of the accursed city and people." Jesus said, "There shall not be left here one stone upon another, that shall not be thrown down." Matthew 24:2. Titus, however, was so charmed by the grandeur of the temple that he gave orders to spare it. In the heat of war, however, a soldier seized a brand and, climbing on the shoulders of a comrade, thrust it into a window. Soon the temple, the pride of the Jews, was ablaze. Realizing the tragedy, the Roman prince and general of the army groaned, and "spreading his hands toward heaven, called God to witness that this was not his doing."—*Historian's History of the World*, Vol. 2, p. 196.

Titus rushed in personally and bore away the golden candlestick, the table of shewbread, and the volume of the law. The candlestick was later deposited in Vespasian's Temple of Peace in Rome. A copy of this is still to be seen on the inside wall of the Arch of Titus, erected to celebrate his victory over the Jews. How accurate was the prophecy: "He shall do exploits, and return to his own land." Verse 28. These exploits included the obliteration of the Jewish temple. To show their anger "against the Holy Covenant" (NEB) the Romans erected a temple to Jupiter, "the father of the gods," on the site of the Jewish temple, sacred since Solomon's great dedication a thousand years before.

The destruction of Jerusalem affected tremendously not only the Jews and the Christians but also the empire itself. Three centuries later Rome, "the eternal city," was the object of Barbarian invasion which continued intermittently until the imperial power of the empire expired in A.D. 476. Strange as it may seem, the Roman Senate at that time sent the official emblems of government to the Eastern Empire in Constantinople, saying they had no further use for them. Do we see in this the beginning of the transition from the pagan Rome of the Caesars to the papal Rome of the popes? Verse 30 says this power would "forsake the holy covenant," which the papacy surely did by the introduction of such doctrines as transubstantiation and the sacrifice of the mass into the worship services of the church.

Important as these parts of this great prophecy are, that which follows is even more vital.

16
Daniel Views Rise
of Persecuting Powers

What tremendous vistas of history are packed into a few verses of prophecy! We have already noticed the exactness of this long prophecy of Daniel 11, and some important events in the experience of Julius, Augustus, and Tiberius. It appears that Gabriel goes back into Jewish history in order to outline the movements of Rome in general, which so definitely influenced God's people. In verse 23 reference is made again to the "league" into which the Jews entered with the Romans in 161 B.C. That was an unfortunate step they took, because Judea, a century later, became a mere province of Rome.

It is not unusual for Bible prophecy to double back and repeat certain events, in order to unfold them more definitely. We find the same events recorded in Daniel chapters 7, 8, 9, and in several places in Revelation. So, having brought the reader down to our Lord's death (verse 22), the prophet then carries us back to the time when Rome, then a "small people," began to grow into an empire. From this point the prophecy leads us in a direct line to events that presage the final triumph of God's people and the establishment of the kingdom of glory.

Nothing else is as important to Daniel's people or to any other people as the substitutionary death of the Messiah, "the Lamb of God, which taketh away the sin of the world." In order to impress the importance of the part Rome would play in these world-shaping events, the angel reaches back to the time when the Romans entered into this league in response to a definite request from the Jewish high priest, Judas, in 161 B.C. Having heard that the Romans had conquered Galatia, Iberia, Carthage, and Libya, and that three kings had been subdued—Perseus, Phillip, and Antiochus the Great —the Jews felt they should enter into an "league of friendship" with this rising power. The pact was made in the name of the Roman Senate, says Josephus, and while it looked attractive at first, it proved a tragic move for the Jews. See *Antiquities*, Bk. XII, Chap. X.

Rome's method of conquest, first promising peace then confiscating "the fattest places," is brought to our notice in verse 24. Under the pretense of offering protection, they gradually moved in to steal the liberties of the world. But as we noticed before, it was "even for a time." Verse 24. Recognizing that a "time" in prophecy equals a year of 360 days, it is interesting to note that from 31 B.C., the year in which Egypt capitulated, until Constantine moved his seat of government from the city of Rome to Constantinople in A.D. 330, makes exactly 360 years.

Dramatic changes were taking place in the Roman Empire. A truce between Constantine in the West and Lucinius in the east lasted from 314 to 323, and then war broke out anew. Lucinius was defeated in 324, and this left Constantine the head of the empire. Byzantium was now in the hands of Constantine, who decided to make this city his capital. He practically rebuilt the city, beautifying it in every way. He intended to call it New Rome, but he was urged to insert his own name; so it became the metropolis of Constantine, Constantinople.

Verse 29 says, "It shall not be as the former, or as the latter." Rome had conquered Egypt "the former" and Judea "the latter." The setting up of this new seat of authority was unique and certainly did not help to stabilize the empire, because on Constantine's death the empire was divided among his three sons—Constantine II, Constantius, and Constans. In the ensuing two centuries this contributed to the collapse of the 500-year empire of Rome.

Constantine Accepts Christianity

With the so-called conversion of Constantine, a new era began for the church. The emperor bestowed favors on the bishops, for he was eager to secure their power for the state. The church and the state united, and paganism insinuated itself into the church. An observer watching the service could scarcely realize it was a Christian worship, for many forms of pagan ritual were carried out. Against this apostasy the Arian Goths rose up and invaded the city of Rome. Gibbon says, "Their arms spread desolation or terror from the columns of Hercules [Straits of Gibraltar] to the south of the Nile."

While Constantine professed to accept Christianity, apparently he was never really a Christian at heart. While a member of the church, his attitude to the church seemed to be motivated solely by political ambitions. It was a sad day for Christianity when the emperor became the chairman of church councils as Constantine was at the Council of Nicea. Though appearing under the cloak of friendship, his heart was really "against the holy covenant." Verse 28.

"The ships of Chittim shall come against him." Chittim ("Kittim" RSV) doubtless refers to the strong maritime power which began to develop in North Africa. Genseric, the clever admiral of the never-defeated navy of the Vandals, was for fifty years their hero. He was the terror of Constantinople and Rome. Carthage became a stronghold from whence he ventured forth with his ships to attack what he said were "the dwellings of men with whom God was angry." Twice Genseric destroyed the Roman fleet, once in the harbor of Cartagena, Spain, and another time off the coast of Carthage itself. Rome was eventually taken and sacked in A.D. 455.

The breakup of the empire of the Caesars opened the way for the establishment of the papacy, which did indeed "pollute the sanctuary of strength." Verse 31. In other words, papal worship corrupted the true understanding of Christ as our Intercessor in the heavenly sanctuary. Many teachings such as the doctrine of transubstantiation undermined the doctrine of the finished sacrifice of Christ on the cross. Roman Catholicism claims that "Christ is offered every day on our altars."

The prominent powers of Europe exchanged their paganism for another type of paganism under the name of Christianity. As an example, in 498 Symmachus, a recent convert from paganism, ascended the papal throne. His advance to the pontifical chair was stained with the murder of his opponent. Once on the seat of authority, his first act was to excommunicate Emperor Anastasius. This was hailed by the crowd as evidence that he was now judge in the place of God, vicegerent of the Most High. This language is familiar to those who have read papal decrees. In place of the continual ministry of Christ a human priesthood was established which claimed the power to forgive sins and open the gates of heaven to the transgressor. This was indeed "the abomination that maketh desolate." Verse 31.

"He will win over by plausible promises those who are ready to condemn the covenant." Verse 32, NEB. In A.D. 533 the Eastern Emperor Justinian, eager to make war against the Vandals, sought for the approval and cooperation of the Bishop of Rome. In that year he wrote a letter, which later became official, to Epiphanius. In this letter he called the Bishop of Rome "the Head of All the Holy Churches," and later "the Corrector of Heretics." The Arian Goths, having conquered Rome, were determined to rule. They were subdued, however, by armies ordered by the Pope in A.D. 538. This marks the date for the beginning of the long prophetic period of 1260 years—538-1798—which has been recognized by Bible scholars for almost 200 years.

Faithful Christians and Jews

During those dark years the Jews were persecuted and driven into ghettos, deprived of personal liberty and citizenship. Christians, too, were persecuted. Thousands of them remained faithful to God and His Word and fled into places of seclusion. Many Jews also were faithful to the teachings of their fathers.

The Waldenses trained their own ministers, who went out disguised as carpenters, tinsmiths, and even surgeons. They carried portions of the Bible all over Europe, sharing their faith with those who would listen. They paved the way for such early Reformers as Wycliffe, Huss, and Jerome. As the scripture said, "The people that do know their God shall be strong, and do exploits." Verse 32.

"And they that understand among the people shall instruct many." Verse 33. How true that was! The scripture also says, "Yet they shall fall by the sword, and by flame, by captivity, and by spoil." These terrible persecutions were instituted not by pagans but by so-called Christians—the apostate church under the leadership of prelates and bishops.

The sixteenth-century Reformation followed the introduction of printing into Europe, and the first book printed was the Bible in A.D. 1456.

In this great prophecy of Daniel 11 we see that mighty conflict between good and evil, between the children of light and the powers of darkness. In this we can see the brave deeds of the Waldenses in maintaining the purity of the faith and in spreading the light of truth over Europe amid the spiritual and moral darkness of their time. We can recognize the courage of the Bohemians in maintaining their faith in the face of huge German armies under papal influence. Here is portrayed the endurance of the Lollards, and later the Lutherans, and the martyrdom of the Huguenots of France. The marvelous story of these and other exploits will never be fully told until that great day when the faithful of all ages shall be gathered into the kingdom of our Lord.

Now, "when they fall, they shall receive a little help." Verse 34, RSV. New legislation began to be passed in a number of countries, which brought some respite. But some, like Tyndale, in order to complete his work of translating the Bible, were compelled to flee to Holland. Persecuted peoples began to leave Europe for America, which became a haven of refuge. But during those terrible years of persecution, the church was being purged and made white, "even to the time of the end." Verse 35. This is the second mention in Scripture of the time of the end. In chapter 7:25 we notice that the apostate church would hold the dominant position in Europe for 1,260 years. This time period lasted from 538 to 1798. The Napoleonic wars brought an end to papal dominance, for on February 11, 1798, Pope Pius VI was taken prisoner by General Berthier of France. In that same year, 1798, the French Revolution came to an end. After two terrible years of the "reign of terror," during which time much blood was shed, tremendous change came into the government of France. The American Revolution had occurred a few years before, and those two revolutions sounded the death knell of "the divine right of kings." The papal power which for more than a thousand years had been leading into captivity was now taken into captivity, fulfilling the prophecy of Revelation 13:10.

In the previous chapter of Revelation the same perod of papal persecution is brought to view, where the church symbolized by a woman fled into the wilderness and was sustained by the Lord. In this very prophecy we notice that the earth helped the woman, opening its mouth and swallowing up the flood which the dragon, or the devil, cast after her. Led by Martin Luther, the Protestant Reformation inflicted wounds in this apostate system by "the sword of the Spirit, which is the word of God." Ephesians 6:17. The Protestant cause was espoused by some of the German states, which gave protection to the Reformers. The work of persecution was also restrained. Queen Mary of England, "Bloody Mary," was a mortal enemy of the Protestant cause, and her relentless persecutions were responsible for the death of many, including the Reformers burned at Smithfield.

A New Era of Toleration and Enlightenment

Certain decrees of toleration were passed in a few countries in Europe prior to 1798. Yet it was not until the nineteenth century dawned that multitudes began to enjoy toleration and even freedom of religion. The Scriptures call this the "time of the end." And it was indeed the end of wholesale European persecutions and the beginning of a freer society. During the later decades of the eighteenth century, under the impact of the evangelical revival, a new world opened up to hundreds of thousands. John Wesley and his brother Charles, George Whitefield, John Fletcher, and others brought about prison reform and education for children. Sunday Schools where children could learn the truth of salvation were opened. This time also marked the beginning of a world mission program which aimed to carry the gospel to every land of earth.

In 1793 William Carey, "Pioneer of Modern Missions," arrived in India. A few years later, in 1804, the British and Foreign Bible Society was organized; and in 1816 the American Bible Society had its beginning. Within a few years Robert Moffat went to Africa, Robert Morrison to China, Adoniram Judson to Burma, John Williams to Polynesia, Allan Gardiner to South America, and David Livingstone to Africa. Thus began the great program of world evangelism so well-known today. The tremendous changes which took place around the turn of the century have played a great part not only in the world's culture but also in our understanding of the world's culture; and, most important, our understanding of the Word of God.

17
The Atheistic Revolution

The section of Daniel's prophecy to which we now turn is the most challenging portion of chapter eleven. Many sincere interpreters have attempted to resolve these verses, but each interpretation seems defective. Take, for example, our Futurist friends, among whom are some of the most dedicated evangelical Christians. They put almost everything into the future, looking for fulfillment *after* our Lord's return, which they believe will be a secret and silent coming. They speak of "the king that shall do according to his will" (verse 36) as the "Willful King," whom they believe will appear as a Jew but who in reality will be "the very incarnation of Satan" —the terrible coming antichrist. They say he will make a covenant with the Jews, but will later persecute them.

Others see in these verses the restored power, the antichrist of the centuries, whose influence and machinations will assume world-wide influence just before Christ's second advent. They point to the similarity of language in Paul's description of the "man of sin" in 2 Thessalonians 2:2-5, also John's prophecy of a worldwide apostate power in Revelation 13:5-8. It seems clear that Daniel, Paul, and John all described the same power. Therefore, they say, it must be the papacy. Still others believe it refers to Russia, or maybe even to Islam. Are all these wrong, or could all be right in some degree?

We do well to observe that verse 36 introduces a powerful personality who, at the time of the end, "shall do according to his own will." Twice previously this prophecy tells of one who will do "according to his will," and each time it signals a dramatic change in the international scene and introduces a *new power*. The first was the lightning rise of the Grecian empire under Alexander the Great. The second was the coming of Rome to world rulership, led by Julius Caesar. Now we meet another who is to do "according to his will."

Who is this one? Some say it is the papacy. While having the greatest respect for those who hold this interpretation, yet there are at least four important questions we must face if we read the papacy into these verses: (1) Was the papacy a *new* power at "the time of the end"? (2) Was the papacy a godless power? (3) Was the papacy ever a military power? (4) Was the papacy able "to do according to his will" at the time of the end, 1798?

Concerning the first question, it is sufficient to say that the papacy was already over a thousand years old at the time and had a long record of persecution and intrigue. Moreover, the ruling pope, Pius VI, was taken prisoner in 1798. He died in Valence, France, on August 29, 1799. Not till March 14 of the following year was a new pope elected.

On the second question the prophecy says: "Neither shall he regard the God of his fathers, . . . nor regard any god." Verse 37. Despite the fact that the papacy corrupted the truth, it was not a godless power.

On the third question, while we admit that certain popes were very active militarily, yet the papacy was not primarily a military power as the prophecy suggests. The Scripture says: "He shall honor the god of fortresses . . . ; a god whom his fathers did not know." Verse 38, RSV. Such words could scarcely be applied to a church. But no words could better describe the atheistic revolution in France during the latter part of the eighteenth century.

The fourth question almost answers itself, for the one power that *could not* do "according to his will" at that time was the papacy. The pope was incarcerated, the forces of atheism having curtailed his power. Atheistic France confiscated the property of the church. The sacred vessels of worship were often melted down for coins, while lead coffins were turned into bullets.

The same atheistic principles which brought to fruition the godless revolution in France are today, however, being taught in schools and colleges everywhere. Ellen White, commenting on conditions

154

at the turn of the century, listed several threats to stable government: (1) centralization of wealth and power; (2) combinations for increasing the wealth of the few; (3) combinations of the poor to defend their interests; (4) "the spirit of unrest, or riot and bloodshed"; (5) "the world-wide dissemination of the same teachings that led to the French Revolution." Then she said of these influences: "All are tending to involve *the whole world in a struggle similar to that which convulsed France.*"—*Education*, page 228 (italics supplied. Note that this speaks of a coming worldwide revolution. At the time these words were written there was little evidence of any such power arising. But a decade and a half later Russia was plunged into her revolution. Since then, the principles of the French revolution have spread to every land of earth. Rather than think of Daniel 11:36-45 as dealing with just the work of the papacy, would it not be wiser to make a wider application? The new world power predicted here and which will finally come to its end will doubtless include the papacy as it will every other apostate and false system of religion. The prophecy also indicates it will be more than just a religious power; it will have to do with commerce and industry as well as with false philosophy. Revelation 18, which is an enlargement of Daniel 11:45, portrays the final collapse of all human government arraigned against God.

Not only is a new and dominant leader introduced in Daniel 11:36, but the prophecy forecasts a new and revolutionary type of government. While the French revolution with all its horror was confined to one nation, it could well be a miniature illustration of the world's final challenge to the living God. That France, the richest, most cultured, and most densely populated country in Europe at that time, could ever become the scene of such brutal disorder and vengeance as stained her record under the later Louis kings seemed impossible. But the unbelievable happened.

The French revolution, however, was but the culmination of two centuries of suppression of the Scriptures, carried out under the guise of religion. Most frightful, heartrending slaughters had been perpetrated, such as the St. Bartholomew Massacre in 1572, which was definitely the work of priests and prelates. Commenting on this, Henry White says: "When the news of the massacre reached Rome, the exultation among the clergy knew no bounds. . . . A medal was struck to commemorate the massacre and in the Vatican may still be seen three frescoes of Tasari, describing the attack."—*The Massacre of St. Bartholomew*, ch. 14, par. 34, quoted in *The Great Controversy*, page 273. Ultimately many voices demanded that in the name of reason religion be abolished. "God does not exist!" they shouted, and the nation through its legislators turned atheistic.

If anyone wonders whether God would bother to mention France in prophecy, the evidence is clear, for the greater part of Revelation 11 deals with the rise of atheism and the French Revolution. "In many of the nations of Europe the powers that ruled in church and state had for centuries been controlled by Satan through the medium of the papacy. But here is brought to view a new manifestation of satanic power."—*The Great Controversy*, pages 268, 269. And "this prophecy has received a most exact and striking fulfillment in the history of France."—*Ibid.* p. 269.

Daniel's prophecy describing the new power that was to arise and do its work in "the time of the end," declares that he would "not regard the God of his fathers," but would "honour the god of forces," or fortresses or munitions. In other words, military power would predominate. Then we should look for some powerful personality, a military genius, who at the "time of the end" would assume authority. Naturally, many see this fulfilled in that military genius Napoleon Bonaparte. Not only did he try to reshape Europe, but he was determined to weld the nations into a single empire. It is said that the word *conscription* was first applied to the armed forces in September, 1798, making men legally liable for service. This made possible a new system of war.

Napoleon was also responsible for many social and economic changes. And historians agree that modern history begins with Napoleon. His rise marked two great revolutions—one in America and the other in France.

The French Revolution had sought to abolish religion, especially the Christian religion, and the Bible. Fouché declared from the pulpit of the cathedral at Vevers that the worship of Reason "should in future be the national religion."—Louis Madelin, *The French Revolution*, page 388. Here surely was "a god whom his fathers did not know."

During the Revolution, in 1793, "the world for the first time heard an assembly of men, born and educated in civilization, and assuming the right to govern one of the finest of the European nations, uplift their united voice to deny the most solemn truth which man's soul receives, and renounce unanimously the belief and worship of a Deity."—Sir Walter Scott, *The Life of Napoleon*, Vol. 1, ch. 17, quoted in *Madelin*, pages 269, 270. "France stands apart in the world's history as the single state which by the decree of her Legislative Assembly pronounced that there was no God. . . . Women as well as men danced and sang with joy in accepting the announcement."—*Blackwood's Magazine*, November, 1870.

Not only did France try to destroy the worship of God among her citizens; she also made divorce easier. One phrase in this prophecy could well relate to that: "Neither shall he regard . . . the desire of women" (verse 37), which theologian Thomas Newton declared could more properly be rendered: "the desire of wives." Other translations read: "nor care for the delight of women," *Fenton;* "the one whom women love,"—*Jerusalem Bible;* "the god beloved of women," NEB. Many interpreters emphasize that it relates to the love of women, particularly conjugal love. In any case, divorce was established in Paris by decree on September 20, 1792, and carried still further by the Convention in 1794. Soon, according to Madelin, "women passed from hand to hand by a legal process" with the tragic result of a very steep rise in illegitimacy.

Christianity Attacked by Atheism

While homes were breaking up, churches were being desecrated. Church bells were melted and cast into cannon. Bibles were publicly burned, and the weekly day of worship was set aside. The Assembly by decree transformed even the famous Notre Dame Cathedral into the *Temple of Reason*. During the "Reign of Terror" which lasted from 1792 to 1794, the Revolution reached its height, and both the church and the government were overthrown. The king and queen and many of the nobility of France were decapitated. An estimated 14,000 people were guillotined.

"Thus shall he do in the most strong holds with a strange god . . . and *shall divide the land* for gain." Verse 39. Previous to the Revolution the Roman Catholic Church and a few landlords owned two thirds of the land of France. The landed estates were confiscated and sold at auction in small parcels; the sales provided much-needed funds for the newly appointed government.

"When the restraints of God's law were cast aside, it was found that the laws of man were inadequate to hold in check the powerful tides of human passion. . . . Peace and happiness were banished from the homes and hearts of men. . . . Violence and lust held undisputed sway. . . .

"The cities of the kingdom were filled with scenes of horror. . . . And to add to the general misery, the nation became involved in a prolonged and devastating war with the great powers of Europe." —*The Great Controversy*, pages 282, 283.

The effort to capture the minds of men began in dead earnest about two hundred years ago with the new religion, so-called, of Rousseauism. Eugene Methvin, in his penetrating analysis, *The Rise of Radicalism*, speaks of a quasi-Masonic secret order known as the Illuminati, "founded in 1776 by Adam Weishaupt, a professor from Ingalstadt and a renegade Jesuit. Weishaupt heartily hated the Jesuits and aimed to replace Christianity with a secular religion of reason."—Page 121. Among the outstanding French leaders was Philippe Buonannoti, who "hailed the French Revolution as the dawning of heaven on earth." It proved to be anything but that, but the ideas inculcated at that time by these radical thinkers is the philosophy behind much of today's world unrest.

"The atheistical power that ruled in France under the Revolution and the Reign of Terror, did wage such a war against God and His holy word as the world had never witnessed. The worship of the Deity was abolished by the National Assembly. Bibles were collected and publicly burned with every possible manifestation of scorn. The law of God was trampled underfoot. The institutions of the Bible were abolished. The weekly rest day was set aside, and in its stead every tenth day was devoted to reveling and blasphemy." —*The Great Controversy*, pages 273, 274.

Six-pointed Philosophy Disrupts France

The corruptive philosophy of Weishaupt and others had done its work in the nation, and the Revolution was the baleful fruit. The atheistic order aimed at nothing less than total world revolution and ultimately a single world government.

Nesta Webster, a British writer, sums up the teachings of the Illuminati in these six important points:

1. Abolition of all ordered government.
2. Abolition of all monarchy.
3. Abolition of all private property and inheritance.
4. Abolition of all patriotism.
5. Abolition of the family (marriage was regarded as outdated and children became the responsibility of the state).
6. Abolition of all religion.

Weishaupt adopted the name Spartacus, leader of an insurrection of slaves in ancient Rome. John Robison, in his book *Proofs of a Conspiracy Against the Religions and Governments of Europe*, published in 1798, declared that Weishaupt's real intention was to "abolish all religions, overthrow every government, and make the world a general plunder and wreck." Patriotism and loyalty were regarded as narrow-minded prejudices. These revolutionary ideas brought on the Reign of Terror, and "they have helped to light the fires of every revolution in the two hundred years since they were published [on May 1, 1776]."—Edward Hodnett, *The Cultivated Mind*, page 27.

The French Revolution was short-lived. The seeds of anarchy, however, spread, ultimately finding fertile soil in Russia, where they devoloped slowly. A century later, in 1917, at the height of World War I, Russia was plunged into the Bolshevik Revolution which embraced many of the principles of the French Revolution.

The steps which led to atheistic-socialism as we know it today are vital. Karl Marx, son of a successful Jewish lawyer who turned Protestant, imbibed these ideas; and with Frederik Engels, a wealthy German Socialist, published the *Manifesto* in 1848. This document echoed ideas of the French Revolution and added a few more. Marx's ideas are credited with having "more impact on mankind than those of anyone else except Jesus Christ."—*Ibid.*

His theories have guided Lenin, Trotsky, Stalin, Kruschchev, and Mao Tse-Tung, and brought half the world under this philosophy. How true is the statement in the book *Education* to which we referred earlier that "anarchy is seeking to sweep away all law, not only divine, but human." And this, we repeat, in combination with unsettling world conditions, is "tending to *involve the whole world* in a struggle similar to that which convulsed France."—*Education*, page 228 (italics supplied). The same writer says: "The enmity of Satan against good will be manifested more and more as he brings his forces into activity in his last work of rebellion; and every soul that is not fully surrendered to God, and kept by divine power, will form an alliance with Satan against heaven, and join in battle against the Ruler of the universe."—*Testimonies to Ministers*, page 465.

At the dawning of the "time of the end," as we have seen, major political changes occurred: the imprisonment of the pope; the French Revolution; the appearance of a new and dominant personality—Napoleon, who said, "There will be no repose in Europe until it is under one head. . . . In five years I shall be master of the world." Describing Napoleon, Mme. de Stael wrote: "This man really does possess the will to shift the world."

Verse 40 declares: "At the time of the end [1798] shall the king of the south push at him: and the king of the north shall come against him like a whirlwind, with chariots, and with horsemen, and with many ships." The king of the north and the king of the south have not been mentioned since verse 16, when we were viewing events occurring about 200 B.C., some 2,000 years earlier.

The king of the south at that time was Egypt, and still is. While Rome ruled Egypt for a short time, that king was still Egypt. Not so with the king of the north. That territory changed hands several times. It was originally the Syrian power. But at "the time of the end" it was under Turkish rule. We might ask, was there conflict between Egypt and France and between Turkey and France at "the time of the end," in 1798? There certainly was. A state of open hostility developed between France and Egypt. Napoleon was planning to invade Egypt at that time, but he declared he was coming only to chastise the Mamelukes for their robbing of certain French merchants. The Mamelukes were the governing class and Napoleon sought to drive a wedge between them and the populace. Furthermore, he cherished hopes of subduing not only Egypt, but Syria, Persia, and India, even as far as the Ganges. These plans he placed before the Directory, and secured their authority for his campaign against Egypt.

He set sail from Toulon on May 19, 1798, with twenty-seven large ships, many smaller vessels of war, and 300 transports. Counting the troops and the ship's crews, probably 50,000 men were involved. On July 2 he took Alexandria. On the twenty-first he fought the Battle of the Pyramids. On July 25 he entered Cairo, the capital. Egypt, able to offer only weak resistance, suffered heavy losses of men and equipment. The words of the prophecy are significant: "The king of the south" shall "push at him"—a feeble resistance. But by contrast, "The king of the north shall come against him like a whirlwind, with chariots, and with horsemen, and with many ships." While this may have some future significance, it certainly had its fulfillment at the "time of the end," for on September 11, 1798, the Sultan of Turkey declared war on France. Thus the king of the south, Egypt, and the king of the north, which at that time was Turkey, both attacked France at the same time.

Napoleon's First Retreat

Napoleon had crushed the armies of Egypt, and he attempted the same thing with the Turks in Syria. A strong body of Turks, however, had entrenched themselves at Saint Jean d'Acre, and thousands of Muslim had gathered on the hills of Samaria. Just at that time Sir Sydney Smith arrived at Saint Jean d'Acre with a small fleet of English ships. His men, aided by Turkey, captured Napoleon's siege equipment.

The siege lasted some weeks, but Napoleon, seeing the situation was hopeless, sounded a call for retreat. On May 21, 1799, he began to retrace his steps toward the territory of the king of the south. But, as the prophecy declared, he was not through. This military genius had one ambition, to unite the world and make himself supreme ruler.

The historian Guizot says of Napoleon, "In his secret thoughts, powerful and chimerical, he nursed the hope of pushing forward to Constantinople, seizing the city, and making himself master of Europe by attacking it from the eastern side. *It was to the conquest of the world* that he marched in advancing against Jaffa."—*Nations of the World*, "France," Vol. 6, p. 388 (italics supplied).

Thiers, another French historian, says: "To penetrate into those countries of light and glory, where Alexander and Mahomet had conquered and founded empires, to make them ring with his name, and to have it sent back to France repeated by echoes of Asia, was for him a most ravishing prospect."—*Thiers' History of the French Revolution*, page 769.

It is unfortunate that in recent times there is a tendency on the part of some to minimize the importance of this period, especially Napoleon's campaigns. But the Napoleonic wars and the French Revolution mark one of the great turning points of history. These events presaged a new era not only for Europe, but for the world.

When the armies of France, led by Napoleon, were defeated, Palestine once again became a small part of the sprawling Ottoman Empire and remained so for the next hundred years until General Allenby, in 1918, won his decisive victory on the age-old Palestinian battle field of Megiddo. That hastened the end not only of World War I, but also of the Ottoman Empire. For his oustanding military leadership Allenby was given the title "Earl of Megiddo."

Since then the political face of the Midde East has changed tremendously. Europe, too, has undergone drastic changes. Between 1914 and 1918 four great empires collapsed—the Russian Empire under the Czars; the German Empire under the kaisers; the Austrian Empire under the Hapsburgs; and the Ottoman Empire, under the sultans. Yes, we live today in a different world from that in which our grandfathers lived. But these changes were all foreseen by the prophet Daniel, who set forth clearly the conditions marking "the time of the end," one of the most imposing being the movement toward world government.

In identifying the power spoken of in the last verses of Daniel 11 it would appear wise for us to look for a larger power than the papacy. Here are 21 points of identity listed in the prophecy, not more than half of which could possibly relate to the papacy, but every one either has been or could well be fulfilled by worldwide atheistic socialism:

1. This power manifests itself "at the time of the end," 1798.
2. Shall exalt "and magnify himself above every god."
3. Shall "prosper till the indignation be accomplished."
4. Shall "speak marvelous things against the God of gods."
5. Shall not "regard the God of his fathers."
6. Shall not regard "the desire of women."
7. Shall not "regard any god."
8. Shall "magnify himself above all."

9. Shall "honour the God of forces," ("munitions," mar.).
10. Shall "honour with gold, and silver, and with precious stones."
11. Shall "cause them to rule over many."
12. Shall "divide the land for gain."
13. Shall "enter also into the glorious land."
14. The king of the south shall "push at him," and the king of the north shall "come against him."
15. He would "stretch forth his hand also upon the countries."
16. He would have power over the treasures of Egypt.
17. The "Libyans and the Ethiopians shall be at his steps."
18. "Tidings out of the east and out of the north shall trouble him."
19. "He shall go forth with great fury to destroy."
20. "He shall plant the tabernacles of his palace" in Jerusalem.
21. "He shall come to his end, and none shall help him."

Some interpreters apply these verses to antichrist which they declare will appear *after* our Lord's return, that is, after the great resurrection. But Daniel 12 makes it clear that the willful king, or the antichrist, makes his attack on God's people prior to the standing up of Michael and the ushering in of the time of trouble, before our Lord's return. Just before that grand event Satan will make a desperate effort to delude the world. He will come "with all power and signs and lying wonders," 2 Thessalonians 2:9-12. "The last great delusion is soon to open before us. Antichrist is to perform his marvelous works in our sight."—*The Great Controversy*, page 593. A world church in collaboration with a world government could easily pave the way for this display of Satan's power.

The Rise and Spread of Marxist Ideas

Six or seven decades ago worldwide socialism was regarded as a wild idea in the minds of a few revolutionaries. When Nicolai Lenin, in 1916, announced that it would conquer the world, such a thing seemed impossible. But the plan he outlined has been so avidly followed that today the whole world feels the power of world socialism. First Russia was taken over; then, as Lenin predicted, the nations of Eastern Europe—Czechoslovakia, Poland, Hungary, East Germany, Romania, Yugoslavia, and Albania. Then the masses of Asia began to capitulate—China, Mongolia, Tibet, North Korea, and North Vietnam.

Karl Marx's theories have infiltrated every land of earth, affecting society, culture, and religion. Karl Marx, as we noted earlier, was the son of a Jewish lawyer. Having studied law and philosophy, he received his philosophy degree from Berlin University in 1841 and immediately proposed his program of radical socialism. In Paris he met Frederik Engels, and they worked together to produce a number of influential articles and books. In Brussels they joined a mysterious group who called themselves the "League of the Just." These hired Marx to write his famous book *Manifest der Kommunisten* or *Communist Manifesto*, which he finished in 1847. The revolutionary plans Marx advocated were much like those set forth seventy years earlier by Adam Weishaupt in his "Order of the Illuminati."

In his book *Das Kapital* Marx writes of the history of the working-class movement; the idea being to appeal to the underprivileged. These principles are today being published in hundreds of languages around the world. But the ideas advocated are similar to those underlying the French Revolution. What began in Europe as a revolutionary philosophy has today become a worldwide movement and a way of life, shaping the lives of half the human race. At first it opposed all religion, especially Christianity. This resulted in a head-on collision with the church, particularly Roman Catholicism. But today there is distinct change of attitude on the part of both communism and Catholicism.

Pope John Gives New Direction to the Church

Since 1958, with the elevation of Pope John XXIII, there has been a rapid alteration in the Vatican's anti-Bolshevik stand. In some areas Catholicism is no longer the implacable foe of worldwide socialism, but an advocate of coexistence. Both groups are undergoing tremendous change. No longer is communism blatantly atheistic. In the Eighteenth National Convention of the Communist Party in the United States of America, held in New York in April 1966, a plan for a single religious organization set in motion the creation of the "Church of World Brotherhood," the ultimate goal of this project being a global state religion where political and church powers would be one and the same. Such a condition would represent at least a partial return to the old politically controlled church.

If such a union were to materialize, while it would include the papacy, yet it would be far more than a papal program; it would be man's final challenge to the living God. The history of God's faithful men in ancient Babylon might well be a miniature of God's ultimate victory over the world or modern Babylon. In Daniel, chapter 1, we see God's men standing firm in matters of diet. Daniel 2 we see God's ability to foretell the future, triumphing over the knowledge of Babylon. In chapter 3 the worship of God proved victorious over the worship demanded by the king of Babylon. In chapter 4, as the king was sent out to eat grass, we see the rulership of God triumphing over the rulership of Babylon. In chapter 5, God rebukes Babylon's blasphemy, and the Persian conquerors take the city. In chapter 6 we see God triumphing over Daniel's persecutors.

Revelation 18 pictures the final collapse of all false religions, all worldly business and commerce, all shipping and finance under the judgments of God. Even "souls of men" are included in the list which makes up the Babylon—the power that "reigneth over the kings of the earth." Chapters 17 and 18 of Revelation have a significant tie-in with Isaiah 2 and Micah 4, where a great peace movement is depicted which ends in destruction when the Lord God "ariseth to shake terribly the earth." It is important to note here the words in Isaiah 2:3: "Come ye, and let us go up to the mountain of the Lord . . . : for out of Zion shall go forth the law, and the word of the Lord from Jerusalem." While the idea is laudable, these are not the words of God but the words of "many people." (Micah 4:2 says "many nations.") Isaiah continues: "Thou hast forsaken thy people the house of Jacob, because they be replenished from the east, and are soothsayers [spiritualists]. . . . Their land is also full of horses . . . [and] chariots [military equipment]." Verses 6 and 7. "Their land also is full of idols; . . . therefore forgive them not." Verse 8, 9. God says, "Enter into the rock . . . for fear of the Lord, and for the glory of his majesty." Verse 10. Human plans for world peace and world religion will come to naught, for "the Lord alone shall be exalted in that day." Verse 17. The apostle Paul says: "When they shall say, Peace and safety; then sudden destruction cometh upon them . . . ; and they shall not escape." 1 Thessalonians 5:3.

We cannot be dogmatic on certain details of these prophecies, for we are dealing with unfulfilled prophecy, and only after events transpire can we be certain. But the world seems to be shaping up for the final display of anti-God power. Jesus said, "I have told you before it come to pass, that, when it is come to pass, ye might believe." John 14:29. Prophecy is given not to make us expert prognosticators, but rather, intelligent interpreters when the events occur.

The angel Gabriel, however, made it clear to Daniel that the power which *comes to his end* will be a power which has worldwide influence. And his collapse will be the signal for our Lord's return. So we need to be alert and watching. The things we witness today throughout the world are surely the final movements of "the time of the end." We can know that the Lord is at hand. Jesus said, "Be ye also ready: for in such an hour as ye think not the Son of man cometh." Matthew 24:44.

For decades, even centuries, men have envisioned a peaceful united Europe. Two frightful world wars have torn the nations apart. Any superman who could assure the world of real and lasting peace would be hailed as the greatest deliverer of all time. Many Bible students predict the rise of such a world leader. They speak of him as the coming antichrist; they declare that he will accomplish many unbelievable things, as the Scripture declares, even calling down fire from heaven as did Elijah in the days of King Ahab. That such a personality will appear the Scriptures make abundantly clear. While he will appear as a man, he will be more than a man. He will be none other than Satan himself impersonating Christ. Stepping onto the world stage, he will deceive men and nations. In Revelation 16:14 we read that demon spirits will "go forth unto the kings of the earth and of the whole world, to gather them to the battle of that great day of God Almighty." To some extent this is happening now. Occultism in all its varied forms was never so popular as it is today. The scripture says, "He gathered them together into a place called in the Hebrew tongue Armageddon." Verse 16. A socialistic dominated world-state, with headquarters in the Holy Land, is even now envisioned by some.

Daniel also speaks of the rise of such a power, declaring that he "shall *plant* the tabernacles of his palace ["his royal pavilion," NEB] between the seas in the glorious holy mountain." Daniel 11:45. But will his reign endure? On this the scripture is very definite. The angel said, "Yet he shall come to his end, and none shall help him.

And at that time shall Michael stand up, the great prince which standeth for the children of thy people: and there shall be a time of trouble, such as never was since there was a nation even to that same time." Daniel 11:45; 12:1.

God's People Delivered

The "time of trouble" spoken of here will be short, but it will be a period of frightful distress—a different kind of trouble from anything before recorded. The medieval centuries, sometimes referred to as the Dark Ages, were tragic times for both the Jews and the Christians, but the coming of trouble which just precedes our Saviour's return in glory will exceed anything in history. Having finished His work of intercession, our Great High Priest lays aside his mediatorial robes and clothes Himself in the garments of a conquering King. His destroying angels then pour out their bowls of wrath—the seven last plagues—upon the despisers of His grace. It will be a tragic time of judgment, but God's people will be protected in those awful days. "He shall give his angels charge over thee, to keep thee in all thy ways." Psalm 91:11. "There shall no evil befall thee, neither shall any plague come nigh thy dwelling." Verse 10.

Many prophets have spoken of this coming time of turmoil. Jeremiah worried, "Alas! for that day is great, so that none is like it: it is even the time of Jacob's trouble; but he shall be saved out of it." Those last words are surely encouraging—"he shall be saved out of it." Daniel says, "At that time thy people shall be delivered, every one that shall be found written in the book." Daniel 12:1. They are delivered, not because they belong to a certain group, but because their names are written in the book.

Gabriel came to tell Daniel what would happen to his people in the latter days. Daniel 10:14. Daniel's people were, of course, the Jews, and vital things were to happen to Israel in the latter days. Some of these are happening right now, many having returned to the Holy Land. But the greatest thing that could happen to this once-scattered nation would be for the scales to fall from their eyes, and they, with clear spiritual insight, would turn to Jehovah in repentance, accepting "the great prince," Jesus of Nazareth, as their Messiah and prepare to meet Him when He returns in glory. The Scriptures do not indicate that the nation as a whole will do this, yet some of the greatest of the Hebrew prophets envisioned a tremendous turning back to God on the part of Daniel's "people," the Jews, just before the Saviour appears. And among the multitudes who will accept salvation are more than natural-born Jews, because all who turn to God in repentance and accept the grace of God become the children of God, whatever their racial background. "For," says the apostle Paul, "ye are all the children of God by faith in Christ Jesus." "And if ye be Christ's, then are ye Abraham's seed, and heirs according to the promise." Galatians 3:26, 29.

A hundred years before Daniel was born, Isaiah wrote about "the sons of the stranger, that join themselves to the Lord, to serve him, and to love the name of the Lord, to be his servants." Isaiah 56:6. "Even unto them will I give . . . a name better than of sons and of daughters." Verse 5. "For mine house shall be called an house of prayer for all people." Verse 7. Paul speak of "Israel after the flesh." 1 Corinthians 10:18. These are the natural sons of Abraham. But the apostle also speaks of the church made up of all nations as "the Israel of God." So, as already noted, Daniel's people include more than natural-born Jews, for all who love the Lord and through faith accept salvation become "Abraham's seed, and heirs according to the promise." Galatians 3:29.

Whether people are born Jews or members of another race, all are saved in exactly the same way. Through faith we all become part of spiritual Israel. Are you ready, dear friend, for that moment when "Michael [shall] stand up, the great prince which standeth for the children of thy people"? If you have not made that surrender, why not give your heart to Him now? Do not delay; He waits your decision. At this very moment you can pass from death to life. Accept Him as your Saviour now, and be prepared for the "time of trouble" so soon to burst upon the world. Then it will be too late to make that surrender. "Now is the accepted time; behold, now is the day of salvation." 2 Corinthians 6:2.

When you make that choice, your name is written in the book of life, and if you are faithful, you will be protected during the awful days head. Soon our Lord will appear with all His holy angels, and together we will be caught up with all God's saints of all the ages to live with Him forever. May the Holy Spirit lead us all to make that decision now for His name's sake.

18
Could Socialism Lead to World Government?

The end of the eighteenth century saw both the end and the beginning of many things. Not only did 1798 mark the end of the 1,260 years of papal dominance, as predicted in Daniel 7:25 and 12:7; it also was the portent of the industrial revolution and the scientific age, to which we shall refer more definitely in our closing chapter.

It is difficult for us to picture the world as it was 200 years ago. In 1797 the first cast-iron plow was patented. Mechanized farming began to receive great impetus. Not only have our methods of work changed, but also our methods of war have changed unbelievably. To illustrate the tremendous growth of the destructive power of our military weapons today, let us draw on a piece of paper a line not more than half an inch long, and let that represent the power of the one atom bomb that dropped on Hiroshima in 1946. Now draw beside it, if we can, a line to represent our present-day explosive capabilities. To do this we will need a paper that will reach a distance of 167 miles! If we never had anything else to tell us, this would be enough to emphasize that we have indeed reached "the time of the end," "the crisis at the close."

Gabriel's message to Daniel was given in order that God's people, godly Jew and Gentile alike, might prepare themselves to stand in the day of final destruction. And among the messages of the angel none is more vital than the one found from Daniel 11:36 to the end of chapter 12. The angel spoke of a power that would arise in "the time of the end" which would wage an intensive war, not merely for the *bodies* of men, as in the days of slavery and labor

168

camps, but for the *minds* of men; its weapons not military hardware but challenging ideas. The bitterest conflict is where men are hungry, longing for food and freedom, for education and the comforts of life. It is an ideological warfare waged in the name of humanity. Science and education are the watchwords of this new era. Those set on world revolution claim they will conquer the world by winning the minds of men. Since World War II this challenging philosophy has virtually taken control of two continents, and in its march to conquest millions of people have perished.

Atheistic Socialism's Rapid Growth

The growth of these ideas staggers our imagination. Dr. James Ray Smith, in his book *God Still Speaks in the Space Age,* makes some interesting observations. On page 57 he reminds us that in 1903 seventeen persons came together and structured the coming revolution. They had neither guns nor planes, ships nor tanks. They had no arsenal of military weapons. But they had an arsenal of ideas. These ideas they exploded in the minds of peasants and villagers.

In the next fourteen years, from 1903 to 1917, that 17 became 40,000. And with 40,000 they took over Russia! During the next twenty years, from 1917 to 1937, that 40,000 extended their control until they numbered 167 million. Then in the next twenty years, from 1937 to 1957, the 167 million became 963 million. With that in mind, Dr. Fred Schwarz challenges us as Christians by claiming that this philosophy has conquered more people in twenty years than Christians have ever told about Christ and His salvation during nearly 2,000 years!

What is the inspiration behind such growth? Mao Tse-Tung declares in his Red Book, the bible of 850,000,000 people, "Our weapons are not machine-guns, but the ideas of Marxism-Leninism." Yes, these ideas are the background of the ideological war between atheism and theism. Battle after battle is being fought and won, not so much for geographical territory as for the minds and souls of men. Arnold Toynbee expressed it well in *Religion in Life* when he said, "The fundamental conflict is not political but religious."— Cited in *God Still Speaks in the Space Age,* page 60. And Dorothy Sayers declares, "The bottom of it is a violent and unreconcilable quarrel about the nature of God and the nature of man and the ultimate nature of the universe; it is a war of dogma."—*Chaos or Creed*, page 25.

In his book *Das Kapital*, Karl Marx wrote that the idea of his movement was to appeal to the working classes. However, we must never get the idea that communism is merely a movement of the downtrodden masses; it is actually a program planned by power seekers. Nor does it stem from just Moscow and Peking; it is a conspiracy guided by leaders in high places, whose one desire is global conquest. In his *Communist Manifesto*, Marx said in essence that the proletarian revolution would establish the socialist dictatorship of the proletariat. But before that could happen three important things must be accomplished: first, the elimination of all right to private property; second, the dissolution of the family unit; third, the destruction of religion, "the opiate of the people." The result is a worldwide moral collapse. True morals are given to make life happier, not harder. "Divorce and disloyalty are not improvements but reversions to the beastly life that we've supposedly outgrown," says David Redding (*The New Immorality*, page 37). The same writer refers to Aldous Huxley's forecast in his *Brave New World* where he says that the rate of divorce continues to accelerate. "In a few years, no doubt, marriage licenses will be sold like dog licenses, good for a period of twelve months, with no law against changing dogs or keeping more than one animal at a time."—*Ibid.*

The Anti-God War of Today

It is both sobering and challenging to realize that for every person who reads the Bible as the Word of God there are five studying the ideas of Marx and Lenin. Many more millions of mothers are telling their children that God *does not* exist than those who tell them He *does* exist, and that Jesus Christ is the Saviour of mankind. While communism at its heart is basically antireligious, the facts are that in both the U.S.S.R. and the People's Republic of China, the condition of the common people has improved greatly. These better living conditions are constantly appealed to as the evidence of this philosophy's great blessing to mankind.

Strolling along the wide avenues of Leningrad, the old capital of Russia, we were deeply impressed with the building program underway all over that city. The new apartment complexes being erected contrast strangely with the older family housing in Russia. But one of the sad scenes was the famed Kazan Cathedral, which for over 125 years functioned as a great center for the Russian Orthodox Church. It is now "a museum to atheism," its apparent purpose being to set at naught the Christian faith.

The early devotees of this philosophy denounced religion as "the opiate of the people." "The first lie is God," they said. If God Himself is a lie, then the Bible is without authority; it is mere folklore and myth.

The Scriptural account of creation was naturally set aside, and the pseudo-scientific belief that man evolved from forms of life was adopted as "more reasonable." While evolution as we know it today is in a sense new, it has its roots far back in history. The story of man's beginning was a definite part of every ancient religion. But in the eighteenth century men of science probed deeper into both geology and biology, seeking a natural explanation of origins. Eventually they created a "ladder of life" with progressive stages stretching over millions of years. The more complex animals, including man, naturally belonged to the last stage. The Bible story of creation was rejected and ridiculed, and in its place the Goddess of Reason was tacitly accepted.

"The time of the end" was marked, therefore, by the rise not only of military might but also by sweeping changes in philosophy, science, and religion. Rationalism, claiming reason as a superior source of knowledge, laid aside what men called the "musty records of the past" as they sought for a new understanding of earth's origin. This resulted in the loss of faith. How relevant is our Lord's rhetorical question, "When the Son of man cometh, shall he find faith on the earth?" Luke 18:8.

While atheism and infidelity have existed in the minds of certain philosophers throughout history, these philosophies are today being taught in the classrooms of high schools and colleges all over the world. In thousands of books and magazines, by programs on television and radio, the theory of man's evolution, as opposed to the Bible account of creation, is being presented as if it were a proved fact.

The Marxist doctrine of "economic determinism," better known as the "class-struggle theory of history," is the underlying principle of textbooks on political science and is the basis of the "social gospel" now being preached from many pulpits. Atheistic socialism, the direct fruitage of the French Revolution, has nothing to fear from such sermons.

Atheistic Socialism Undergoing Change

One of the most interesting changes is in world socialism itself. No longer do we find the fierce opposition to religion as at the beginning. Instead there is often a friendly, tolerant attitude. Roman Catholicism's present stand on the question of economic determinism is also very enlightening. The Vatican seems no longer to be anti-Bolshevist, but now advocates coexistence, as indicated by some recent significant moves. This changed attitude on the part of Catholicism is in itself a revolution; through her long history the Catholic Church has taught that she is the one and only door to heaven. Her present leaning toward neopaganism, so prominent in the emphasis of the World Council of Churches, is therefore difficult to believe. She is changing also in other respects, making it easier for nations and denominations to accept her leadership.

According to Bible prophecy, when the papacy has fully recovered from the "deadly wound" inflicted by the state in 1798, she will play a vital role in the closing scenes of earth's history. Nor will she be alone, for John in the symbolic prophecy of Revelation 17 pictures a woman riding a scarlet-colored beast, and in her person she bears the "names of blasphemy." This symbolism is well understood by Bible students, for in prophecy a woman represents a church, and a beast a political power. So in this prophetic picture we see a great political power being guided by a corrupt church. And in verse 14 we read: "These shall make war with the Lamb [Christ], and the Lamb shall overcome them: for he is the Lord of lords, and the King of kings: and they that are with him are called, and chosen, and faithful."

The next chapter unfolds the final collapse of a great religio-political colossus. Revelation 18:8-24. These verses seem to be an enlargement of Daniel 11:45. How the books of Daniel and Revelation complement each other!

While dealing with unfulfilled prophecy we must be cautious.

Yet it appears that politics, economics, and religion will ultimately combine to bring about the long-envisioned "world government," which was the basic idea of Weishaupt's Illuminati. Doubtless many and varied influences would play a part in bringing such a program to fruition. It is even possible that the newly created Common Market could become an important factor. Jean Monnet, father of the Common Market, said, "As long as Europe remains divided it is no match for the Soviet Union. Europe must unite." —*Look*, November 26, 1966. Servan Schrieber declared that "a successful response to American technology, organization, and research demands a united European effort."—*New York Times Magazine*, May 19, 1968.

It is claimed that this proposed united Europe could outstrip the U.S.A. or the U.S.S.R. in power and prestige, leading the way to the long-dreamed-of world government. The apparent objective of all this may be international peace, a laudable aim. But the apostle says that at the very time when the world will be proclaiming "peace and safety," then "sudden destruction cometh upon them . . . ; and they shall not escape." 1 Thessalonians 5:3. It is not that God does not desire peace among the nations, but until men's hearts are changed there can be no lasting peace.

The Coming of the Indispensable Man

Socialism is not the answer to the world dilemma. Human ingenuity is insufficient to meet our need, whether it be an energy crisis, a political crisis, a financial crisis, or a religious crisis. Only the coming of the Son of Man, the Indispensable Man, the God-Man, can bring the peace for which all men hope and pray.

19
Righteous Shine
as the Stars Forever

"At that time shall Michael stand up, the great prince which standeth for the children of thy people." These opening words of Daniel's last chapter are deeply significant. The previous nine verses picture events leading to the creation of a great world government. This masterful attempt of man to govern himself will be his final challenge to the living God.

In Revelation 16:13, 14 the prophet John speaks of the spirits of demons coming from three great sources—the dragon, the beast, and the false prophet. And the prophecy declares that these powers will gather the whole world "to the battle of that great day of God Almighty." The scripture further states they will be gathered together "into a place called in the Hebrew tongue Armageddon." Verse 16. When that happens, a mighty voice is heard from heaven announcing, "It is done!" or "It is over!"

All is finished. Then the greatest demonstration of organization and power the world has ever known will collapse. For at that time God Himself will step in and take over the rulership of this runaway world. The prophecy declares, "He shall come to his end, and none shall help him." It is then that Michael stands up, "the great prince . . . : and there shall be a time of trouble, such as never was since there was a nation." Daniel 11:45 and 12:1.

Who Is Michael, the Great Prince?

What does the standing up of Michael mean? Is this some intervention of one of heaven's highest angels on behalf of the Palestinian

Jews? No! It is something far greater. Michael is not just one of heaven's highest angels; He is the Archangel whose mighty voice will call the dead to life again. In Jude 9 we read of Michael coming to raise the body of Moses, at which time the devil disputed His authority. But the Archangel Michael issued the divine command, "The Lord rebuke thee!" Note three important words in this brief account: "Michael," "Lord," and "archangel." He who rebuked the devil and raised Moses from the dead is the One who will yet call to life and immortality all who have died in the blessed hope of the resurrection. Talking to Martha, Jesus said, "I am the resurrection, and the life: he that believeth in me, though he were dead, yet shall he live." John 11:25. And at another time, "The hour is coming, in the which *all* that are in the graves shall hear his voice, and shall come forth." John 5:28, 29.

The voice of the Archangel is the voice of the Life-giver. His authoritative command will sound through all the world: "Awake and sing, ye that dwell in dust"; then "the earth shall cast out the dead." Isaiah 26:19. At that time all who have died believing God's Word will toss aside their coverlet of dust and spring forth joyfully into eternal life.

The name "Michael" means "Who is like God?" He is like God because He *is God*—one with the Father from all eternity. More than twenty times in the New Testament we read such statements as "Christ sitteth on the right hand of God" or "sat down on the right hand of God." Colossians 3:1; Hebrews 10:12. At the throne of grace Christ has been officiating as our High Priest, our Intercessor, but someday soon His ministry of intercession will cease. No longer will He occupy the throne of grace, for mercy's door will have closed forever. It is then that He stands up to receive the kingdom and prepares to return to earth for His people.

The Glorious Return of Christ

What wonderful pictures the prophets have given us of our Lord's return! When He comes, it will be in His own glory and in the glory of the Father and in the glory of the holy angels. Note these verses of Scripture: Luke 9:26, Matthew 25:31, 2 Thessalonians 1:7-10, Revelation 1:7.

"At that time thy people shall be delivered, every one that shall be found written in the book," said the angel. Daniel 12:1. They will be delivered not because they are Jews or Christians, not because they belong to a certain group or denomination, not because they are black or white, but because their names are written in the book—the book of life. It will be worth everything in that day to have our names in that book.

During that awful time of trouble there will be a partial resurrection. "Many of them that sleep in the dust of the earth shall awake, some to everlasting life, and some to shame and everlasting contempt." Daniel 12:2. The resurrection spoken of here is not the general resurrection at the time our Lord is seen coming in the clouds of heaven, for then the righteous only are raised. Says the scripture: "Blessed and holy is he that hath part in the first resurrection: on such the second death hath no power." Revelation 20:6. "But the rest of the dead [the wicked dead] lived not again until the thousand years were finished." Verse 5. A short time before our Lord appears, there will be a special resurrection. This is emphasized in Revelation 1:7: "Behold, he cometh with clouds; and every eye shall see him," says John's prophecy, "and they also which pierced him." In Matthew's gospel we read of a special resurrection when our Lord arose from the dead. So again there will be another special resurrection associated with His second advent. At that time those most prominent in their demand that Christ be crucified—those who gave sentence against Him in the judgment hall, crying, "Crucify him!" those who drove the nails through His hands and feet—will come forth from their graves to see Him coming in power and great glory.

When our Lord was arraigned before the Jewish court on trial for His life, the high priest demanded that Jesus tell him whether He was truly the Christ, the Son of God. With calm assurance the Saviour answered, "Yes, I am," or "it is as you say," but He quickly added, "Nevertheless I say unto you, Hereafter shall ye see the Son of man sitting on the right hand of power, and coming in the clouds of heaven." Matthew 26:64.

According to the words of Christ Himself, those who pierced Him, those who mocked and derided Him in His dying agonies, will be raised to witness the coming King of kings and Lord of lords returning in all His glory. And not only many wicked, but also many righteous will be raised, for the scripture says, "some to everlasting life, and some to shame and everlasting contempt." Daniel 12:2. Could there be anything more thrilling for those who have faithfully proclaimed God's last great message to the world than to come forth from their dusty beds to witness their Saviour returning as conquering King accompanied by all the holy angels? Ellen G. White speaks of those who have died in the faith of the third angel's message as coming forth "to hear God's covenant of peace."—*The Great Controversy*, page 637.

As the Stars Forever

The promise in the next verse has a special meaning for us today. "And they that be wise ["teachers," margin] shall shine as the brightness of the firmament; and they that turn many to righteousness as the stars for ever and ever." Verse 3. The stars have always attracted thoughtful minds, but in recent years we have learned much about these heavenly bodies. Kingdoms may rise and fall, empires go down to dust, but the stars in their stately orbits shine on from century to century. Some are so far away that it has taken a hundred million years for their light to reach us. The wise, said the angel—teachers of God's message of righteousness—will shine as those radiant orbs for all eternity.

Are you planning to be among them, dear friend? You can be, if you accept God's gift of righteousness. "Messiah the prince" is still our ministering Intercessor in the heavenly sanctuary. Through His abundant grace all may become members of His family, and the promise is that we shall shine "as the stars for ever and ever."

Having finished his great prophecy, Gabriel now tells Daniel to "shut up the words, and seal the book, even to the time of the end," implying that many things the prophet did not understand would at that time be understood. Then Daniel overhead one asking the question, "How long shall it be till the end of these wonders?" And the answer came from the one clothed in linen, "It shall be for a time, times, and an half." That, of course, is the same period mentioned in chapter 7, verse 25—the 1,260 prophetic days or years which began in A.D. 538 and ended in 1798. At that time many things not understandable in Daniel's day—nor could they be until the expiration of that period—would come into sharp focus. Even though the great prophet himself said, "I heard, but I understood not" (verse 8), yet we who live in the time of the end can understand. How privileged we are!

What Are We Seeing Today?

Jesus said, "Blessed are your eyes, for they see: and your ears, for they hear. For verily I say unto you, That many prophets and righteous men have desired to see those things which ye see, and have not seen them; and to hear those things which ye hear, and have not heard them." Matthew 13:16, 17. "Blessed are your eyes, for they see"! If Christ were speaking in person to us now, He would be able to say the same thing: "Blessed are your eyes . . . and your ears."

This striking stanza from Bishop Arthur Coxe's "Hymn for the Times" (1842) might well have been penned this very decade:

> "We are living, we are dwelling
> In a grand and awful time,
> In an age on ages telling—
> To be living is sublime.
> Hark! the waking up of nations,
> Gog and Magog to the fray;
> Hark! what soundeth? Is creation
> Groaning for her latter day?"

As the angel closed his message to Daniel, he said, "Knowledge shall be increased." The accuracy of this needs no emphasis. Think of the hundreds, the thousands of things we use which were unknown and undreamed of at the beginning of the time of the end —nuclear power and space travel, for example. The increase of knowledge is not only in science but also in Biblical studies. In 1799, at the beginning of "the time of the end," the Rosetta Stone was unearthed by Napoleon's soldiers when stationed on the banks of the Nile. Deciphering that stone was a difficult task, but it gave scholars new tools to decipher other ancient artifacts. Numerous points of Bible history have been confirmed as a result—knowledge which has helped to confound the claims of the school of rationalism. Much more truth is understood today because of the increase of knowledge in both sacred and secular history.

Daniel's Book Unsealed to the Righteous

Daniel, still eager to understand, asked, "O my Lord, what shall be the end of these things?" Again the voice answered, "The words are closed up and sealed till the time of the end" (Daniel 12:8, 9), or "till the crisis at the close." Moffatt. While "none of the wicked shall understand," yet "the wise shall understand," said the angel. And understanding, they become teachers of truth, preparing a people to endure in the great day of the Lord. At that time all nations will be convulsed, and the unprepared will flee in terror, calling for the mountains and rocks to bury them. They cannot endure that blazing vision of glory as they see Jesus riding forth in power, with all the holy angels, to deliver His people. Having defied the living God and given their allegiance to Satan, they will at last be compelled to witness the disintegration of their colossal world government.

In anticipation of that collapse, those who love God and His truth will through the power of the Holy Spirit "be purified, and made white, and tried," that is, refined. They will separate from every form of worldliness and idolatry and, accepting by His grace Christ's robe of righteousness, will abide "under the shadow of the Almighty" while the earth rocks to ruin. In the midst of crashing skyscrapers and shaking mountains, they will sing to the glory of God: "Therefore will not we fear, though the earth be removed, and though the mountains be carried into the midst of the sea; though the waters thereof roar and be troubled." "The Lord of hosts is with us; the God of Jacob is our refuge." Psalm 46:2, 3, 11.

Daniel's book closes with the mention of two prophetic periods —the 1,290 days and the 1,335 days. Verses 11, 12. The 1,290 days or years might well have begun with the alliance of the church and state under King Clovis of France in 508. From that important event the period then would reach to the time of the end, 1798. The 1,335 days, being an addition of 45 days or years, could bring us to 1843, when the great advent awakening reached its height.

Inasmuch as Gabriel was commissioned to make Daniel understand what would befall his people the Jews in the latter days, some have wondered if the 1,335 prophetic days or years might refer to the *Hegira*, or the Muslim era, which was exactly 1,335 lunar years. The *Hegira* began with the flight of Mohammed in A.D. 622 and

would thus end in 1917, a short time before World War I ended
and the Ottoman Empire collapsed. The last coins minted for the
old Turkish government, one of which is in the possession of the
writer, bears the date 1917, and on the reverse side in Arabic num-
erals, 1335!

The Middle East Awakens

The collapse of the Ottoman Empire, which for centuries had
ruled that area of the world, gave new opportunity not only to the
Jews as a nation, but led to tremendous changes in the whole Middle East. Little did anyone realize how vast were the oil fields in
that part of the world. Lands which for centuries existed in poverty
suddenly became wealthy beyond computation. And riches have
meant power to these peoples. Additional light will doubtless be
shed on the 1,290 and 1,335 days, for "the path of the just is as the
shining light, that shineth more and more unto the perfect day."
Proverbs 4:18. Till we get more light, we do well to keep alert and
watch for God's providences.

The angel's last words to Daniel were, "Go thou thy way till the
end be: for thou shalt rest, and stand in thy lot at the end of the
days." Daniel 12:13. Moffatt translates it, "Go and wait for the
end; you shall rest in the grave and then rise to enjoy your share
at the end of the days."

Some might ask, "Where is that grave that entombs the remains
of the great prophet?" Charles Boutflower says that by common
consent Jews, Sabeans, and Mohammedans declare that the prophet's body lies close to the acropolis in Shushan, or Susa, near to the
place where he received the great vision recorded in chapters 10-12.
He further states that when Abu-Musa-Alashari invaded Persia in
AD 640, it is reported that he sent word to the Khalif Omar that
when he entered the castle he found a chamber under lock and
key. On entering, he saw a stone coffin wrapped in gold brocade
in which was the body of a man of great stature. Inquiring who this
might be, he was told that the people of Iraq, among whom he lived
till the day of his death, called him Danyel Hakim, "Daniel the
sage." "When Omar heard the story, he ordered that the body in
the coffin be reverently buried where the people of Shushan could
no longer have access to it. Accordingly the stream which supplied

the city with water—apparently a canal cut from the Ulai—was diverted, and a grave made in the dry channel; after which the waters were allowed to flow over the body of Daniel."—Charles Boutflower, *In and Around the Book of Daniel,* pages 223, 224.

Where the body of that great prophet actually lies is a matter of interest, but not of particular importance. He rests only till the great resurrection day, when the righteous dead will come forth immortal and glorified.

What a day of victory that will be when Christ, the great Conqueror, comes to claim His people! Accompanied by all the armies of heaven, He sweeps down the vaulted skies in the full panoply of His celestial greatness. Amid clouds of fire and pillars of smoke He descends in power and great glory in full view of all the people of the earth. Mountains melt. Hills skip like lambs, and the seas roll back in majesty as the voice of the Life-giver, like peals of crashing thunder, summons the sleeping saints. What a sight to behold as these radiant ones, rising from their dusty beds, some even from the oceans, spring forth bearing the bloom of eternal youth!

Overcome and frenzied with fear, kings and slaves, mistresses and maids rush alike, seeking desperately for shelter from the blazing presence of Him whom they have despised. They shriek in terror, "The great day of his wrath is come; and who shall be able to stand?" Revelation 6:17. Says the scripture: "Our God shall come, and shall not keep silence: a fire shall devour before him, and it shall be very tempestuous round about him. He shall call to the heavens from above, and to the earth, that He may judge his people." Psalm 50:3, 4.

Daniel will certainly be among those resurrected saints, for the last message of the angel Gabriel to that man of God was both a promise and a triumph: "Thou shalt rest, and stand in thy lot at the end of the days," or "You shall arise to your destiny at the end of the age." NEB. Would that all of us, reader and author alike, might close our life record with such a ring of heavenly assurance. And each of us can, by the grace of God. Someday soon, if faithful, we will share with Daniel and the righteous of all the ages the eternal joys of the life to come. In the presence of Him who became the Son of man that He might make us sons and daughters of God, we shall praise His holy name forever and ever. Amen.

BIBLIOGRAPHY

Abbott, Walter M. *The Documents of Vatican II.* New York: The American Press Book Publishers, 1966.

Abyderus. *On the Assyrians,* page 86.

Anderson, Albert W. *The Battle for Freedom.* Washington, D.C.: Review and Herald Pub. Assoc., 1949.

——————. *Through Turmoil to Peace.* Warburton, Australia: Signs Publishing Co., 1932.

Berkouwer, Garrit C. *The Conflict With Rome.* Philadelphia: The Presbyterian and Reformed Pub. Co., 1958.

Batoli, Giorgio. *The Primitive Church and the Primacy of Rome.* London: Hodder and Stoughton, Ltd., 1907.

Bauman, Louis S. *Russian Events in the Light of Bible Prophecy.* New York: Fleming H. Revell Co., 1942.

Bettanson, Henry. *Documents of the Christian Church.* London: Oxford University Press, 1845.

Bevan, Anthony A. *A Short Commentary on the Book of Daniel for the Use of Students.* Cambridge: The Cambridge University Press, 1892.

Birks, T. R. *The Four Prophetic Empires.* London: Seely, Burnside and Seely, 1845.

Boettner, Loraine. *Roman Catholicism.* Philadelphia: The Presbyterian and Reformed Pub. Co., 1968.

Boutflower, Charles. *In and Around the Book of Daniel.* Reprint. Grand Rapids, Mich.: Zondervan Publishing House, 1963.

Carr, William Guy. *Pawns in the Game.* Glendale, Calif.: St. George Press, 1967.

——————. *The Red Fog Over America.* St. George Press, 1972.

Chemnitz, Martin. Translated by Fred Kramer. *Examination of the Council of Trent.* St. Louis, Missouri: Concordia Publishing House, 1971.

Criswell, W. A. *Expository Sermons on the Book of Daniel.* 3 vols. Grand Rapids: Zondervan Publishing House, 1968, 1971.

Dobbs, Zygmund and Archibald Roosevelt. *The Great Deceit.* West Sayville, N.Y.: Veritas Foundation, 1964.

Driver, Samuel R. *Bible Old Testament Daniel.* Cambridge: The Cambridge University Press, 1922. (The Cambridge Bible for Schools and Universities, Vol. 23.)

Eidersheim, Alfred. *The Life and Times of Jesus the Messiah.* Grand Rapids, Mich.: Wm. B. Eerdmans Pub. Co., 1962.

Elliott, Edward B. *Horae Apocalypticae.* London: Seely, Burnside and Seely, 1847.

Eusebius (Bishop of Caesarea). *A Commentary on the Apocalypse.* Andover, Mass.: Moses Stuart, Allan Morrill and Wardwell, 1845.

Free, Joseph R. *Archaeology and Bible History.* Wheaton, Ill.: Van Kampen Press, 1950.

182

Froom, L. E. *The Prophetic Faith of Our Fathers*. 4 vols. Washington, D.C.: Review and Herald Pub. Assoc., 1946.

Gaebelein, Arno Co. *The Fundamentals*, Vol. 11. Chicago: Testimony Pub. Co.

Gibbon, Edward. *The History of the Decline and Fall of the Roman Empire*. 7 vols. New York: Harper and Brothers.

Grattan, Guiness. *Romanism and the Reformation*. London: J. Nisbet and Co., 1891.

————. *The Approaching End of the Age*. London: Hodder and Stoughton, 1882.

Guizot. *Nations of the World*.

Hefele, Charles Joseph. *A History of the Church Councils*. Edinburgh: T. and T. Clark, 1896.

Herts, J. A. *The Pentateuch and the Hoftorahs*.

Hislop, Alexander. *The Two Babylons*. Edinburgh: James Wood, 1862.

Hodgkin, Thomas. *Italy and Her Invaders*. 9 vols. Oxford: Clarenden Press, 1892.

Horn, Siegfried H. and Lynn H. Wood. *The Chronology of Ezra 7*. Washington, D.C.: Review and Herald Pub. Assoc., 1970.

Hiscox, Edward T. Author of *The Baptist Manual*. Paper read before New York Minister's Conference. Printed in *Source Book for Bible Students*. Washington, D.C.: Review and Herald Pub. Assoc., 1919.

Hodnett, Edward. *The Cultivated Mind*. New York: Harper & Row Publishers, 1963.

Hoover, John Edgar. *Masters of Deceit*. New York: Holt, Rinehart & Winston, Inc., 1958.

Jastrow, Morris. *Religion of Babylonia and Assyria*. Boston: Ginn & Co., 1898.

Jerome. *Commentary on Daniel*. Translated. Grand Rapids: Baker Book House, 1958.

Josephson, Emanuel M. *Roosevelt's Communist Manifesto*. New York: Chadney Press, 1955.

Josephus, Flavius. *Antiquities of the Jews*. Translated. Edinburg: Thomas Nelson & Sons, 1837.

————. *Wars of the Jews*.

Keil, Karl Friedrich. *Book of Daniel*. Vol. 23 of his Biblical commentary on the Old Testament. Grand Rapids, Mich.: Wm. B. Eerdmans Pub. Co., 1949-60.

Keller, Werner. *The Bible as History*. London: Hodder & Stoughton, Ltd., 1956, 1965.

Kenan, H. S. *The Federal Reserve Bank*. Los Angeles: The Noontide Press, 1968.

Lenormant, Francois. *The Beginnings of History According to the Bible and the Traditions of Oriental Peoples*. Translated from the 2d French edition. New York: C. Scribner's Sons, 1882.

Luther, Martin. *Creeds of Christendom*. Translated.

Madelin, Louis. *The French Revolution*. New York: G. P. Putnam's Sons, 1916.

Manhatten, Avro. *Vatican Imperialism in the Twentieth Century*. Grand Rapids, Mich.: Zondervan Publishing House, 1965.

Martin, Rose L. *The Selling of America*. Santa Monica, Calif.: Fedelis Publishers, Inc., 1973.

Marx, Karl. *The Communist Manifesto*. Translated. New York: Monthly Review Press, 1964.

Mauro, Philip. *The Seventy Weeks and the Great Tribulation*. Boston: Hamilton Brothers. Scripture Truth Depot, 1923.

Methvin, Eugene. *The Rise of Radicalism*. New Rochelle, N.Y.: Arlington House, 1973.

M'Clintock and Strong. *Cyclopedia VIII*. Pages 95, 96.

Nampon, A. (S. J.) *Catholic Doctrine as Defined by the Council of Trent*. Philadelphia: Peter H. Cunningham, 1869.

Newton, Sir Issac. *Observations Upon the Prophecies of Daniel and the Apocalypse of St. John*. London: J. Darby and T. Browne, 1733.

Newton, Thomas (Bishop of Bristol 1704-1782). *Dissertations on the Prophecies*. Northampton, Mass.: William Butler, 1796.

Payne, J. Barton. *Encyclopedia of Biblical Prophecy*. New York: Harper & Row Publishers, 1973.

Preston, Robert L. *Wake Up America*. Salt Lake City: Hawkes Publications, 1972.

————. *The Plot to Replace the Constitution*. Salt Lake City: Hawkes Publications, 1972.

Pritchard, James B. *Ancient Near Eastern Texts*. Princeton: Princeton University Press, 1955.

Pusey, E. B. *Lectures on Daniel the Prophet*. Oxford: John Henry and James Baker, 1864.

Rawlinson, George (1812-1902). *Ancient History From the Earliest Times to the Fall of the Western Empire*. Rev. ed. New York: P. F. Collier and Son, 1900.

Redding, David A. *The New Immorality*. New York: Fleming H. Revell Co., 1967.

Robison, John. *Proofs of a Conspiracy Against the Religions and Governments of Europe*. Originally printed in Edinburgh in 1798. Belmont, Mass.: Reprinted by Western Islands, 1967.

Richards, H. M. S. *One World*. Washington, D.C.: Review and Herald Pub. Assoc., 1972.

Sayers, Dorothy Leigh. *Chaos or Creed?* New York: Harcourt, Brace & World, Inc., 1949.

Schaff, Philip. *The Creeds of Christendom*. Vol. 1. Grand Rapids, Mich.: Baker Book House, 1919.

Schlegel, Friedrich von (1772-1829). *The Philosophy of History*. New York: D. Appleton & Co., 1841.

Schroeder, H. J. *Cannons and Decrees of the Council of Trent*. London: Queen Square, 1941.

Scott, Sir Walter. *The Life of Napoleon Bounaparte, Emporer of the French*. Philadelphia: Carey, Lea and Carey, 1827.

Smith and Cheetham. *A Dictionary of Christian Antiquities*. London: John Murray, 1880.

Smith, James Ray. *God Still Speaks in the Space Age*. Grand Rapids, Mich.: Baker Book House, 1967

Smith, Uriah. *Daniel and the Revelation*. Washington, D.C.: Review and Herald Pub. Assoc., 1944.

Smith, William. *A Dictionary of the Bible*. New York: Fleming H. Revell Co.

Taine, Hippolyte A. (1828-1893). *The Modern Regime*. Translated by John Duranc. New York: H. Holt & Co., 1890-94.

Tanner, Joseph. *Daniel and the Revelation*. London: Hodder and Stoughton, 1898.

Tatford, Frederick. *The Climax of the Ages*. Grand Rapids, Mich.: Zondervan Publishing House, 1964.

Thiers, Adolphe (1797-1877). *The History of the French Revolution* 3d American ed. Philadelphia: Carey and Hart, 1842.

Tregelles, S. P. *Remarks on the Prophetic Visions in the Book of Daniel*. London: Samuel Bagster and Sons, 1883.

Webster, Nesta H. *The French Revolution*. London: Constable and Co., Ltd., 1919.

————. *World Revolution: The Plot Against Civilization*. Boston: Small, Maynard & Co., 1921.

White, Ellen G. *Christ's Object Lessons*. Oakland, Calif.: Pacific Press Pub. Co., 1900.

————. *The Desire of Ages*. Pacific Press Pub. Co., 1898.

————. *Education*. Pacific Press Pub. Co., 1903.

————. *The Great Controversy*. Rev. ed. Mountain View, Calif.: Pacific Press Pub. Assoc., 1911.

————. *Prophets and Kings*. Pacific Press Pub. Assoc., 1917.

————. *Testimonies for the Church*. 4th ed. Pacific Press Pub. Assoc., 1948.

————. *Testimonies to Ministers*. Pacific Press Pub. Assoc., 1923.

White, Henry, *The Massacre of St. Bartholomew*. 1871.

Williams, Henry Smith, ed. *The Historians' History of the World*. 25 vols. London and New York: The History Association, 1907.

Young, Edward J. *The Prophecy of Daniel*. Grand Rapids, Mich.: Wm. B. Eerdmans Pub. Co., 1949.

Abomination of desolation 117
"Abomination that maketh
desolate" 149
"Abraham's seed," believers as 167
"According to his will," signifi-
cance of 152, 153
Advent awakening 95, 96
Adversus Christianos, Porphyry's,
basis of rational criticism 31
Ahasuerus (Xerxes), wealth and
reign of 131
Alexander the great 153
builds the Grecian Empire
49, 50, 90
career of 90, 131
influence of Daniel's prophecies
on 29, 30
Alexandrian library, destruction of
138
Allenby, General, conquers
Palestine 161
America, persecuted Europeans
fled to 150
American Bible Society organized
151
American Revolution 150
Antichrist, prediction of, as world
leader 165
work of, before Christ's return
162
Anti-God war of today 170-172
Antiochus Epiphanes, discussion of
103, 104
Antiochus III, the Great 133
Apocalyptic prophecy introduced
by Daniel 13
Aramaic, part of Daniel written in
36
Arbela (Gaugamela), battle of 90
Arch of Titus 115
Archaeology, Daniel's record
confirmed by 35, 36
Archangel identified 175
Arian Goths subdued by pope 149

Aristotle, tutor of Alexander 49,
90
Ashurbanipal, famous library of
17
last strong king of Assyria 14
Ashur-uballit, last king of Assyria
14
Assyria, final collapse of 17
Astrologers, magicians, and philosophers in Chaldean school
of science 24
Astronomy, Babylonian 25, 26
Atheistic revolution, the 152-167
Atheistic socialism, as king of the
north 161, 162
changes in 172, 173
rapid growth of 169, 170
Augustus (Octavius), rise of
139, 140
Austrian Empire, collapse of 161

Babylon, city of, rebuilding of
27, 28
fall of, to Cyrus 81, 82
history and glory of 47, 48
Babylonian Empire, founding of
17
Bear, symbol of Medo-Persia
38, 89
Beasts, meaning of 88
Belshazzar, as last king of Babylon
36, 39
coregent with Nabonidus 87
major point of attack by critics
36
Belshazzar's feast 77-80
Berthier, French general, takes
Pope Pius VI prisoner 52,
53, 95, 150
Bible, a book of prophecy 33, 34
Bible printed in 1456 150
Bohemians, courage of 150
Bolshevik revolution, seeds of, in
French philosophy 158

Book of the law, discovery of   15
Brass (bronze), symbol of Grecian
    Empire   48, 49
British and Foreign Bible Society
    founded   151
Bronze, Greeks used   49

Caesar, Julius   153
Carey, William, missionary to India
    151
Catholic support for Common
    Market   52
Catholicism, change in attitude of
    toward communism   172
Cestius, siege of Jerusalem by   115
Chaldean invasions of Judah   13,
    14
Chaldeans, governing class in
    Babylon   24, 25
Challenge, man's final, to the living
    God   164
Changing God's times and laws   93
Charlemagne, attempts of, to
    reestablish empire   51
    founds Holy Roman Empire   105
Charles V, attempts of, to unite
    Europe   51
Christ, baptism of   114
    ministry of, as High Priest   122,
    123
    our Judge   100
    public ministry of   119, 120
    return of   58, 59, 175-177
    the stone   55, 56
Christian, King, of Denmark, as
    grandfather of royalty   57
Christianity, attacked by Atheism
    156, 157
    spread of, aided by Roman law
    and system   50
"Chittim, ships of"   148
"Church of World Brotherhood,"
    proposal for   163
Civilization, contribution of
    Babylonians to   25, 26

Clay, feet of, meaning of   50
Cleansing of sanctuary   122, 123
Cleopatra, career of   137
Common Market, goal of, to unite
    Europe   52, 53, 173
Communism, change in attitude of,
    toward religion   172
    success of   170, 171
Communist Manifesto, production
    of   163
    program of   170
Constantine, career of   147, 148
    conversion of   105
Constantinople made capital of
    Roman Empire   147
"Corrector of Heretics," Justinian
    calls pope   149
Council of Nicea, Constantine as
    chairman of   148
Critics, attack of, on Belshazzar
    36, 37
    on book of Daniel   31-40
    four challenging questions for
    38, 39
Cyaxeres I, king of Medes, alliance
    of, with Babylon   17
Cyrus, overthrows Babylon   37,
    81, 82
    prophecies concerning   80, 81
Daily, the, meaning of   105, 106
Daniel, chief of wise men   24-26
    as eunuch in Babylon   28
    as prophet and statesman   13,
    29
    book of, written partly in
    Hebrew and partly in Aramaic
    36
    Christ's estimate of   29
    comparison of, with Joseph   22
    education of   15, 16
    grave of   180, 181
    included in death decree for
    wise men   43
    influence of, on Greek history
    29, 30
    long career of   18

probable birth date of   14
reads handwriting on wall   37
prominent features about   23, 24
recognized by Christ as prophet   13, 29
refusal of royal cuisine by   20
Sir Isaac Newton's estimate of   29
supposed tomb of, in Susa (Shushan)   19
taken into exile   14
unusual place of, in history   13

Daniel, book of, classed with Jewish pseudepigrapha   32
Josephus on authorship of   29
Darius the Median   82, 83
Das Kapital, Karl Marx's book   170
"Deadly wound," papacy receives   53
Decrees, three, for rebuilding Jerusalem   111-113
"Desire of women"   156
Diet, results of following plain   20
Divorce, acceleration in rate of   170
results of, in French Revolution   156
Dream, Nebuchadnezzar's, of metal image   43-61
Dura, plain of, image on   62-67

Economic determinism, Marxist, taught in schools   172
Egypt, how Rome gained control of   137-139
Judah's dependence on   17
Elephantine papyri, Aramaic of, similar to Daniel's   36
Enlightenment, new era of   151
Enlil, chief god of Sumerians, replaced by Marduk   59, 60
Empires, collapse of four great   161

Europe, attempts to reunite   51-53
Evolution, belief in, basic to communism   171
Ezekiel, mentions Daniel as righteous   19
probable site of exile of   27
taken into exile   14
Ezekiel's estimate of Daniel   26, 27
Ezra, work of   112, 113

Four beasts, prophecy of   87-96
Four kings of Daniel 11:2, identification of   130, 131
France, as the power of Dan. 11:36-38   153, 154
atheism in   153-159
French Revolution, conditions under   154-159
Futurist interpretations of prophecy   152
Futurists, views of   119
Gabriel, message of, to Daniel   166, 168
Gardiner, Allan, missionary to South America   151
Gaugamela (Arbela), battle of   90
Genseric, Vandal chief   148
German Empire, collapse of   161
German rationalism, anti-Christian philosophy of   31, 32
Goat and ram, prophecy of   101, 102
God, Daniel's vision of   126
God's people delivered   166, 167
Gold, head of, meaning of   45
Golden image on plain of Dura   62-67
Greece, brass (bronze) as symbol of   48, 49
rapid conquest of Persia by   49
Grecian Empire, divisions of   90
Greek language used for spread of gospel   50

Habakkuk, prophecies of, foretold
  rise of Chaldeans   18
Handwriting on wall   78-80
  read by Daniel   37
"Head of all the Holy Churches,"
  Justinian calls Bishop of
  Rome   149
Head of gold, meaning of   45
Hegira, Mohammed's   179
Hiddekel, identification of   125
Hiroshima, atom bomb on   168
Hitler, attempts of, to conquer
  Europe   51
"Holy covenant," Constantine
  against   148
Holy Roman Empire, founding of
  105
Huguenots of France, martyrdom
  of   105
Huss   149

Ideological warfare   169
Illuminati, basic idea of   173
  teachings of   158
Indespensable Man, coming of
  173, 174
  only, can bring peace   173
Inquisition   92
Iron, symbol of Rome   50
Isaiah, prophecies of, foretold rise
  of Babylon   18
  about Cyrus   80, 81
  about eunuchs in Babylon   28
Israel, failure of, to fulfill God's
  purpose   41, 42, 46, 47

Jehoiakim, foolish policy of   17
Jeremiah, attempts of, to reform
  Judah   16
  prophecy of, concerning seventy
  years captivity   28
Jerome   149
Jerusalem, destroyed by Titus
  104, 115, 116, 144, 145
  God's original purpose for   46

rebuilding of   111-114
  siege of, by Nebuchadnezzar
  17
Jesus, use of prohecy by   34
  weeps over Jerusalem   115
Jews, form "league of friendship"
  with Rome   146, 147
  persecution of, during "Dark
  Ages"   149
  salvation for   166, 167
John the Baptist, preaching of
  118
John XXIII, Pope, influence of
  163
Joseph, comparison of, with
  Daniel   22
Josiah, reign of   15
Judah, made vassal state by
  Nebuchadnezzar   17
Judea, a Roman Province in
  63 BC   135
Judeo-Christian religion, depen-
  dence of, on prophecy   33, 34
Judgment, description of   97, 98
Judson, Adoniram, missionary to
  Burma   151
Julius Caesar, career of   137-139
Justinian, campaign of, against
  Vandals and Goths   149

Kaiser William II, attempts of, to
  conquer Europe   51
King of the north, Turkey as   159
King of the south, Egypt as   159
Knowledge, increase of   178
Kozan Cathedral, a museum to
  atheism   171

Layard, discovered of Ashurbani-
  pal's library   17
"League of friendship" with Rome
  by Jews'   146, 147
Leopard, symbol of Grecia   89, 90
Library of Ashurbanipal   17
Little horn (Daniel 7), identifica-
  tion of   91, 92

Little horn (Daniel 8), identification of   102-104
Lion, symbol of Babylon   89
Lions' den   84, 85
Livingstone, David, missionary to Africa   151
Louis XIV, attempts of, to rule Europe   51
Luther, Martin, Protestant Reformer   151

Magi, origin of   24
Mamelukes, ruling class in Egypt 159
Mao Tse-Tung   169
Maruk (Merodach) becomes chief god of Babylon   59, 60
Marx, Karl, work of   158, 163
Mary, "Bloody" Queen, persecutions of Reformers by   151
Massacre of St. Bartholomew   154, 155
Mathematics, advanced, of Babylonians   26
Medes, allies of Babylon against Assyria   17
Medes and Persians overthrow Babylon   37, 38
Medo-Persia, ram as symbol of   38
   bear as symbol of   38
   troops of, take Babylon   80
Melzar, chief steward in charge of Hebrew captives   20
Mene, Mene, Tekel, Upharsin 78-80
Messiah, anointing of   114
   "cut off"   115
   the "Lamb of God"   146
Messianic ministry proved by prophecy   34
Michael, identification of   127, 128
   standing up of   166, 167, 174, 175
Mission, program of world   151

Moffat, Robert, missionary to Africa   151
Money, Hebrew word for, same as for silver   48
Morrison, Robert, missionary to China   151
Mountain, stone becomes a great 59
Mystery cult, Babylon as center of 48

Nabopolassar, death of   14
   made king of new Babylon   17
Nabonidus, last king of Babylon 36, 37, 39, 77, 87
Nabunaid Chronicle   37
Napoleon, attempts of, to rule Europe   51, 53
   career of   155, 156
   Egyptian campaign of   159, 160
Napoleonic Wars   95, 150
Nebuchadnezzar, acknowledges Daniel's God as supreme   61
   argument over spelling of   35
   assumes throne of Babylon   15
   campaigns of   14
   conversion of   73-75
   crown prince of Babylon   14
   golden image of   62-67
   loses his reason   72
   made Judah a vassal state   17
   treatment of Daniel and companions by   19, 20
   rebuilding of Babylon by   27, 28
Nehemiah, work of   113
New era of toleration and enlightenment   151
Nicea, Council of, Constantine as chairman of   148
Nimrod, Babylon founded by   48
Nippur, center of Babylonian religion before Nebuchadnezzar 59
Nineveh, fall of, to Babylon   17

North, king of   131-134
Nuclear power   168

Octavius (Augustus), rise of   139,
    140
1,260 days (years), prophecy of
    94, 95, 149, 150, 177-180
1,335 days (years)   179, 180
Ottoman Empire, collapse of   161,
    180

Paganism enters Christian church
    147, 148
Papacy, as power of Dan. 11:36-38,
    153
    rise of   148
Pax Romana   50, 142
Peace and safety—sudden destruc-
    tion   173
Peace and safety, vain hopes for
    164
Persecuting powers, rise of   146-
    151
Persia, silver as symbol of   48
Persians and Medes overthrow
    Babylon   37, 38
Pompey, defeat of, by Caesar   137
Pope taken prisoner by French
    95, 150, 153
Porphyry's attack on Christianity
    31-33
Prayer, Daniel's   109, 110
Preterists, views of   119
Prophecy, denial of, by critics   32
    genuine, unique to Bible   33
    God's claim set forth in   33
Protestant Reformation   95, 149-
    151
Protestant Reformation inspired by
    prophecies   118, 119
"Pulse," Daniel's request for   20
Pydna, battle of, significance of
    49, 50
Pyramids, battle of   160

Ram and goat, prophecy of   101,
    102
Ram, symbol of Medo-Persia   38
Reason, Temple of   156
Rationalism replaces orthodox faith
    in God   171
Reign of Terror   156, 157
Reformation, mention of   149-151
Resurrection day   181
Resurrection of righteous   175,
    176
Resurrection, special, before
    Christ's coming   176, 177
Revelation 17 and 18, relation of,
    to Daniel   172
Rock, Scriptural symbolism of   55,
    56
Roman Empire, breakup of   148
    divided by Constantine   147
    divisions of   51, 91
    dramatic changes in   147
    power of   104
Roman roads aid Christianity   50
Rome, bishop of, recognized by
    Justinian as "Head of all the
    Holy Churches"   149
    iron as symbol of   50
    Jews make "league of friendship"
    with   146, 147
    rising power of   135, 136
    rules the world   49, 50
Rome's method of conquest   147
Rosetta Stone   178
Russian Empire, collapse of   161

Salamis, Persians defeated at   131
Sanctuary, cleansing of   106, 107
"Sanctuary of strength," pollution
    of   148
Satan, meaning of   127
Scarlet-colored beast   172
Scientific age, beginning of   168
"Seal the book"   177
Septuagint (LXX), translation of
    133
Seven last plagues   166

Seven words of prophecy prevent united Europe 51

Seventieth week, important events of 121, 122

Seventy weeks, prophecy of 111-117

Seventy years captivity foretold by Jeremiah 28

Sexagesimal system 63

Shadrach, Meshach, and Abednego 19, 63-67

Shadu Rabu, "a great mountain," applied to Marduk 60

Shushan, Daniel in 101

"Small people," Rome as 146

Smithfield, Reformers burned at 151

Social gospel, relation of, to Marxist class-struggle theory 172

Socialism not answer to world dilemma 173
spread of 162, 163

Son of man, "coming" of, in Daniel 7 99

South, king of 131-134

"Spartacus," name adopted by Weishaupt 158

St. Bartholomew Massacre 154, 155

Stephen, martyrdom of 120

Stone, great image shattered by 54, 55, 59

Summachus, acts of, as pope 148

Sunday Schools, opening of 151

Synagogue, origin of, during Babylonian captivity 28

Syria, a Roman province in 65 BC 135

Syrian Wars 132-134

Temple of Reason 156

Ten kingdoms, names of 51

Ten-horned beast, symbol of Rome 90, 91

Tiberius, successor to Augustus 141

"Time" in prophecy 147

Time of Christ's coming, when to expect 57, 58

Time of the end 150, 151, 177, 178
political changes in 159

Time of trouble 166, 167

Titus, Jerusalem destroyed by 115, 116

Toleration, new era of 151

2,300 days (years), prophecy of 106, 107, 123

Tree, dream of 70, 71

Twelve hundred and sixty days (years) 94, 95, 149, 150, 177-180

Tyndale, work of 150

Tyre, siege of, by Nebuchadnezzar 69

Vandals harrass Rome 148

Victoria, Queen, as grandmother of royalty 57

Waldenses, work of 149, 150

Weishaupt, philosophy of 157, 158

Wesley, John and Charles 151

"When God Wants a Man" (poem) 22, 23

"Willful King" concept 152

Williams, John, missionary to Polynesia 151

Wise men, Chaldean "scientists" as 24

Wise men, failure of, to interpret king's dream 42

Wise men, purpose of, in court of Babylon 42

World peace, vain hopes for 164

World revolution, march of 169

Wycliffe 149

Xerxes (Ahasuerus) wealth and reign of 131